Out of Ireland

OUT OF IRELAND
A reading of Yeats's Poetry

by Dudley Young

A CARCANET PRESS PUBLICATION

First published 1975
by Carcanet Press Limited
266 Councillor Lane
Cheadle Hulme, Cheadle
Cheshire SK8 5PN

Printed in Great Britain
by W & J Mackay Limited, Chatham

PREFACE

This book began many years ago as a thesis for Cambridge University and I have many debts to acknowledge. My Cambridge masters were John Beer, Donald Davie, Ronald Gray, Tom Henn and Raymond Williams. At Essex University I would thank John Barrell, Gordon Brotherston, Herbie Butterfield, Tim Clark, George Dekker, Carey Harrison, Jack Hill, Rosamund Lomax, Alasdair MacIntyre, Stanley Mitchell and Gabriel Pearson. Further afield are Michael Black, Juliet Cashford, Northrop Frye, Tom Hadden, Robert Lowell, Tom Parkinson, Charles Rycroft and Val Warner. This list represents various kinds and degrees of generosity, much of it critical of the paths I chose to take, and I trust each person will take his appropriate share of my gratitude; and yet I must thank Donald Davie above all, for the sort of friendship without which this book would not have found its form.

A great deal has already been written about Yeats, and though much of it is nonsense, some of it genuinely illuminates this very difficult and very intelligent poet. Like every student of his poetry I have been helped by this literature, and the reason I refer infrequently to it in the present volume is that my concern is with Yeats, not his critics, and this concern has produced quite enough footnotes as it is. (A comprehensive guide to the critical literature can be found in Jeffares's *Commentary on the Collected Poems.*) I should also mention that *Out of Ireland* assumes a considerable familiarity with Yeats in the reader, and he will need a copy of the *Collected Poems* if he is to follow my arguments: the subtitle of this book means what it says.

The notation used to identify the quotations can be decoded in the bibliography, which lists the works cited in the text. All dates bracketed after poem titles indicate the year of composition, except in the case of 'The Grey Rock' where the date is that of publication, because the date of composition is uncertain.

Finally, acknowledgements are due to M. B. Yeats, Esq., Miss Anne Yeats, the Macmillan Company of London and Basingstoke, the Macmillan Company of Canada and the Macmillan Publishing Company, Inc., for permission to quote from the following works by Yeats: *Collected Poems* (Copyright Macmillan Publishing Company, Inc., 1956), *Collected*

*

In the twentieth century, the American voice has sounded with increasing authority in the English-speaking world. The best minds of Allen Ginsberg's generation were destroyed by the madness they perceived in the western mind, and the best of my generation were devastated by the fallout over Vietnam. Is the silence which now pervades the west an indication of our terminal folly, or may it gesture, for some at least, towards a rebirth of wonder? This book, a meditation on the best mind of the twentieth century's first generation, on the way he took on the madness and may have survived, is offered in the hope of some therapy for that madness, and is dedicated to the fallen.

Abberton, Essex
1975

CONTENTS

All the arts when young and happy are but the point of the spear whose handle is our daily life. When they grow old and unhappy they perfect themselves away from life, and life, seeing that they are sufficient to themselves, forgets them.

W. B. Yeats

Why should we celebrate
These dead men more than the dying?

T. S. Eliot

ces humeurs transcendentes m'effrayent . . .

Montaigne

But the lot of 'em, Yeats, Possum and Wyndham
had no ground beneath 'em.

Ezra Pound

INTRODUCTION

Magic

> The lunatic, the lover, and the poet
> Are of imagination all compact:
> One sees more devils than vast hell can hold,
> That is, the madman: the lover, all as frantic,
> Sees Helen's beauty in a brow of Egypt:
> The poet's eye, in a fine frenzy rolling,
> Doth glance from heaven to earth, from earth to heaven;
> And as imagination bodies forth
> The forms of things unknown, the poet's pen
> Turns them to shapes, and gives to airy nothing
> A local habitation and a name.

(Midsummer Night's Dream)

Shakespeare is still the touchstone of sanity for the English mind, and this passage will bear pondering for some time yet. The speaker's tough-minded mockery of the three principal exponents of imagination assures us that he is no sentimentalist: having thus allayed our suspicions of that dangerous word 'imagination', he then issues a bold declaration on its behalf. In the space of eleven lines we are led from the excesses of lunatic and lover, through the mediating frenzy of the poet's eye, to assent finally in the important business of turning nothing into something.

A book such as this one, asking the reader to think seriously about a poet who claims even more for the imagination than Shakespeare does, written at a time when the poet's frenzy is generally thought even less interesting than the madman's, needs some such defence.

For Shakespeare's poet, imagination is the divine faculty whereby some of the secrets of heaven may be published on earth. In theological terms it is the organ of revelation. Those who find the word 'heaven' fanciful or obscure may at least agree that 'we are such stuff as dreams are made on'; and that it has traditionally been the poet's function to discover and inform his society's dreams, of heaven and hell, of beginnings and endings.

Not just to discover the dreams, however, but through the sorcery of his craft to make them substantial, to register them publicly as significant realities. The angels and the demons which are airy nothings without the poet's magic are *bodied* forth in his verse — that which was not, is, and yet is not. To this one must add that poetic sorcery has also been traditionally used in the opposite direction, to conjure the dead: that which was, and is not, is. Contact with the dead fathers is quite as crucial to a society's life as venturing forth into 'the forms of things unknown'. In short, by giving us access to the past and the future, the poet can offer us some hope of access to the present; and by giving a name to the sublime and the terrible, he gives us a compass to steer by.

Such, at any rate, may be the function of the poet in a society which recognizes his importance. That Shakespeare almost buries his defence of poetry in mockery suggests that he expected some scepticism in his audience. By Yeats's time that scepticism was very much greater: so great in fact that he could believe the wheel had come full circle and that the poet, having been rendered utterly powerless in the materialist ethos of the nineteenth century, was about to retrieve the eminent position he had enjoyed in archaic times. Yeats was encouraged in this belief by his Irishness; for the revival of the old Irish culture which he hoped for as a young man might include the revival of the Gaelic bard (or *fili*), a potent political figure in ancient times:

> The *fili* undoubtedly inherited his magic powers from the *drui* or druid, who must have been more a wizard than a priest; Latin lives of the Irish saints often use the word *magus* to translate *drui*. The fact that the words for 'druid', 'prophet', 'poet', 'judge', and 'physician' are virtually interchangeable in the Early Irish sagas and the lives of Irish saints (in both Latin and Irish) suggests that the druid originally combined the functions of all.[1]

Even when Yeats lost faith in the Irish revival, his poetry remained significantly 'druidic'; and hence some preliminary discussion of the poet as magician is in order.

1. Vivian Mercier, *The Irish Comic Tradition*, p. 107.

The Irish *fili's* political power arose largely because his satirical verses were thought capable of inflicting actual injury upon the satirized. Although Shakespeare's poet may seem by comparison a much less potent figure, his sorcery is of the same kind; and so is Yeats's. The fact that Yeats is addressing a much more sceptical society than Shakespeare makes the question of his magical pretensions one of the first to arise; is he out of step or is his audience? Can one responsibly assert in the twentieth century that imagination *bodies* forth anything at all? I believe not only that one can but that one must. To make the case, however, some background is necessary.

The traditional sorcery of the poet derives from what the anthropologists call 'sympathetic magic', which is universally practised in primitive societies. Its principle is a simple one: by making a copy or an image of a thing, I re-produce its essence, which is the source of its being, which I may then worship, command or destroy. The classic example of this is the sticking of pins in the wax effigy of a foe. The wild animals on the cave walls at Lascaux are now thought to have been painted for magical purposes. And word magic works in the same way; when the Irish *fili* composes satirical verses about his foe, the latter must look to his luck. These three instances are by no means isolated or exceptional examples of a magical function in primitive art; indeed, Gombrich suggests that such is the original function of all art; 'All art is "image-making" and all image-making is rooted in the creation of substitutes.'[2] One should add that various 'arts' today manifest fairly crude magical intent; unpopular figures are often burnt in effigy, not always as whimsically as Guy Fawkes; painters such as Francis Bacon are trying to tame our nightmares much as the Lascaux cavemen did; and the gods are still asked to damn all sorts of things.

To practise magic is essentially to make contact with and harness supernatural powers. This is manifestly a dangerous undertaking, which may explain why many magical practices depend for their success upon the scrupulous performance of a more or less elaborate ceremony or ritual. The ritual both arouses the god's attention and placates his anger, thus providing a channel through which the sacred power may be

2. E. H. Gombrich, *Meditations on a Hobby-horse*, p. 9. Gombrich's main concern is the visual arts but he suggests analogies with the verbal arts in his first chapter.

12

safely conducted into the profane world. In many cases (such as the Christian mass) the ritual imitates the occasion by which contact with the god was originally made. Thus, just as the effigy is a re-presentation of the foe, so the ritual is a re-presentation of the original bridge between the sacred and the profane. Indeed, the affinity between ritual and magic is such that Lévi-Strauss can say 'all ritual tends toward magic'.[3] When one considers that such arts as painting, sculpture, poetry, music and drama all originated in ritual contexts, one sees nothing strange in the fact that artists have often been thought sacred, and not radically different from priests and magicians.[4]

But surely, one may object, this account of sorcery still leaves us a long way from the word-play of a Shakespeare or a Yeats. In fact the distance is not great, and can be covered by a brief consideration of classical epistemology.

As the ancient Greek philosophers were moving the western mind from magical to rational modes of thought, they came upon a problem which remains as central and perplexing today as it was then. It is called the problem of universals and concerns the relations of sameness and difference. All knowledge depends on the ability to perceive the relation of sameness; for example, in order to know that the proposition 'This is a chair' is true, I must be able to perceive that this object and the concept 'chair' bear a relation of sameness one to the other. But are any two things really the same? If so, in what does their sameness consist? For example, what is it that any two chairs have in common which enables us to recognize them as two different instances of the same thing? It cannot be a sameness of material, or of shape; if they are the same, it must be that they bear some formal, structural resemblance to each other, express the same idea — (the idea of 'a thing to sit on'). In short, if there is to be an actual chair there must be some invisible idea or form of Chairness which it imitates or belongs to, along with every other chair that ever has existed, will or might exist. So Plato argued; and though the notion of a heavenly realm of Eternal Ideas struck even him as somewhat primitive, it inaugurated 'Realistic' metaphysics and continues to perplex philosophers today.

3. *Totemism*, p.57. For a similar approach, see Mary Douglas, *Natural Symbols* London, Barrie & Rockliff, 1970, p.10.

4. An etymological note: the word 'magic' comes through Greek and Latin from the Persian *Magu*, the name for a member of the Medean and Persian priestly caste.

The only honest alternative, grasped by Heraclitus, is to deny sameness altogether, and say something like 'Everything is what it is and not another thing' (or what he actually said, 'You cannot step twice into the same river'). This is called Nominalism, and in the end it is as disturbing, for without universals we cannot know anything. In between these two positions comes Conceptualism, which has tried, in a well-meaning liberal way, to reconcile their differences. The differences, however, resist liberal compromise, and we are left with the dilemma: either the mind can perceive sameness (and therefore use concepts to know the world) or it cannot. If it can, then we are forced to believe in a mysterious realm such as Plato describes. In short, the ground of knowledge is itself unknowable.

I realize that those readers not already familiar with the problem of universals will not have grasped it in the preceding paragraphs; and they will have to take my summary on trust. To those who would like a fuller account I recommend the lucid prologue to I. A. Richards's *Beyond.* However, a complete understanding of this, the oldest problem of philosophy, is not necessary for present purposes. The important point is that at the very heart of western rationalism there is a mystery or riddle; and that for all our sophistication we are, after 2,500 years, still more or less stuck with Plato's Forms. This fact is not nearly as well known as it should be, doubtless because the philosophers who tend it have little inclination to advertise their inability to get free of their shadowy beginnings.

The point needs stressing. Sympathetic magic and rational knowledge are two different ways in which man tries to deal with his world. We have been taught (by Sir James Frazer *et al.*) to believe that they are radically different, the first primitive and silly, the second civilized and sensible. This is not true. They are different ways of operating with the relation of sameness, which is the basic and mysterious ground of all purposive mental activity. As for efficacy, they each have their proper sphere: rational philosophy and the modern science it has spawned are obviously the more potent; but we are now beginning to pay for the extent to which this potency has blinded us to some of our primitive obligations, such as the enduring need to propitiate the gods of nature. But that is another story.

In *Totem and Tabu* Freud welcomed Tyler's definition of magic as 'the mistaking of ideal connections for real ones'. Now that we are free from the Victorian orthodoxy that magic is just bad science for primitives, we should amend this to 'the taking of ideal connections for real ones', or 'the making of connections through symbolic representation'. As such it will cover both the primitive's wax effigy and the philosopher's 'This is a chair'.[5]

The philosopher's interest in his proposition may be like the primitive's interest in his effigy, in which case he wants in the end to increase his active power over chairs (to build them, to burn them, to buy them or sell them). But there is another possibility: he may simply want to 'know' them, in and for themselves. This possibility was basically not available to the primitive, and its discovery in the west is generally credited to Plato when we say that it was he who commended to us philosophy as the *dis*interested love of knowledge. Indeed, it was the view of both Plato and Aristotle that contemplative knowledge (*sophia*) was of a higher and worthier kind than practical knowledge (*phronesis*); that is to say, stronger magic. It, too, finds its vindication in the theory of ideas, and is of particular importance to the present argument as it represents a development of sympathetic magic on which most poetry as we know it is based.

When Plato says a chair gets its chair-ness from participating in or imitating the idea of chair, it will soon occur to one of his students (whose country cousins were perhaps still practising sympathetic magic in the Attic hills) that simply to possess the idea of chair might well give him some power over individual chairs, which after all derive their identity (their being, their reality) from imitating this idea. It stands to reason that the idea or type has more importance, reality or power than any instance or token of it.

In a sense this is sympathetic magic in reverse, and logically this should make it the more powerful; for the savage who constructs an effigy possesses only the token of the type which is his foe. If the token, which is derivative, is to influence its source, it needs some outside help: hence the gods must be ritually invoked. It is rather like the child who needs

5. The pin and the doll are ideally connected and this is taken really to connect pain and the foe. In the philosopher's case, the words 'this' and 'chair' are ideally connected, and this is taken really to connect the object in question with the idea Chair.

a weapon if he is to hurt his father. The contemplative philosopher on the contrary, aspires to be like the father who has nothing to fear from his children, and stares upon their reality which is but an imitation of his own.

If one then grants that the student at Plato's Academy who possesses the idea of Chair might think he possessed something powerful, one must then ask, powerful in what sense? What can he do with his idea? The answer to this must be 'Nothing at all. He simply enjoys the wonder of possession'. The moment the student can assent to this he becomes a lover of *sophia*; and Plato is pleased. The *vita activa* has cancelled itself and passed over into the *vita contemplativa*. The new-found philosopher will henceforth consider the practical interests of his country cousins (including what he will learn to call their black magic) vulgar. Henceforth he will seek to unite his mind to all the Forms — not just the chair and the table but all the way up to the good and the beautiful. In the end he hopes to possess all of reality, in effect become God; but he has no wish to act upon the world, only to wonder at things that are as they are.

It is somewhat crude to say that Plato invented contemplative word-magic, since the poets and the pre-Socratic philosophers in Asia Minor were arguably practising it before him. But his doctrine of the Forms gave it a theoretical basis, and his lyrical language in praise of contemplation has inspired philosophers and poets to go and do likewise ever since.

It remains to show how this philosophical activity also commends itself to the poets, particularly since Plato wanted to banish them from his Republic. The original function of Homer's poetry was quite practical: it was to conjure on ceremonial occasions the spirits of the dead fathers, the mythical originators of Greek civilization, for counsel and benediction. The Homeric party in fourth-century Athens (including the sophists) would argue against Plato that the exploits of the old heroes in fact represent what he calls the Form of the good and the beautiful, and that the utterance of Homer's words can bring them to mind; and that even when one had become too 'rational' to seek ritual counsel and benediction in this way, one could summon them merely for the pleasure of possessing them. In short, even when the Homeric poems had lost their religious function in Greek life, one could cherish them as fitting objects of contemplation.

Plato would not agree to this, not least because he held that poetry does not provide the proper tools for quarrying the Eternal Forms. In his view philosophical discourse was the way, since God was a philosopher. Against this one can maintain that God has always been primarily a poet, and that the best way to know him is to learn his native language. This dispute is still with us today, and the only point I would make here is that poetry is ritualized language whereas prose is not, and to that extent has always been a more credible avenue of approach to the sacred.[6]

A good way to grasp the nature of poetic magic, and to appreciate its relation to the philosophical sort, is through its basic tool, metaphor. The philosophical conquest of the world proceeds through classification, i.e. the bringing of a hitherto unknown X into the circle of knowledge by seeing its similarity to an already known Y through the proposition 'all Xs are Ys'; for example, the man who first finds a platypus egg can announce, after some reflection, that all duck-billed platypi are mammals. The primitive poet proceeds in a similar way, for he too is concerned with perceiving sameness where it was not hitherto perceived, in order to increase power. Thus when the poet-priest declares that tribe A is the fox and the moon whereas tribe B is the fish and the sun, he is telling the tribes how they differ, where their power resides, where to focus their totemistic activities, and so on.

As the philosopher and the scientist take over a culture's classification, the poet's assertions become metaphorical; that is, they no longer proclaim *identities* between Man and Nature but only resemblances. For example, when the primitive Greek poet says 'An angry man is a roaring lion', this means that the man actually becomes a lion, participates in the Form of leoninity. But when the culture no longer looks to the poet for such definitions, the statement can only mean that an angry man behaves in a similar fashion to a roaring lion. To discover what anger *really* is we look to the psychologist, and these days he tells us that it is drive-acceleration; and of course the psychologist is right. Henceforth when a man is invaded by the leonine he will feel like a high-revving machine, and we can expect the culture to be modified accordingly. The poet may go on saying that anger is *like* a roaring lion, but we

6. Poetry is not the only contestant, of course. Anyone who cares deeply for music will tell you that God is unquestionably a musician.

who know it is drive-acceleration can only smile at the pretty epithet and agree that poets are idlers and fantasists.

In short, when the poet must settle for metaphor, his magical powers are in decline. In the case of western culture, this has meant that we have come to experience ourselves and the world as machinery instead of living substance — a cliche' of Romanticism but none the less true for that. The implications are serious because the major human experiences, of birth and death, of duty and love and virtue, cannot be registered meaningfully as mechanism; and without them a culture collapses, as ours has.

But this is common ground. In addition to the fall into metaphor there are two other developments of particular importance to the fate of poetry between the time of Plato and the passage from Shakespeare with which we began. First, from Christianity, the belief in historicity: that is, the belief that reality and the human condition are not eternally the same, but develop through history. Secondly, from the Renaissance, the disappearance of God. The first of these developments means that the Eternal Ideas change or unfold; and if revelation is a continuous process, the poets, as technicians of the sacred, will soon become more concerned with uncovering the future than preserving the past through contact with the dead fathers. The second, the disappearance of God, ultimately means the collapse of belief in a supernatural order. But gods do not vanish in an instant, they wither away; and as they wither their priests are forced to discard humility and find the godhead in themselves. Individualism, self-intoxication, fantasy and whimsy are the result, until finally poetry itself is discredited.

Both of these developments can be discerned in the Shakespeare passage. First, no mention of the poet's traditional concern with preserving the past; instead we are offered 'the forms of things unknown'. There is no suggestion that these things have resided eternally in some Platonic heaven; they have been created *ex nihilo*, from 'airy nothing'. Secondly, God is not mentioned, and the supernatural words are used ironically: hell is a vast tank full of tadpoles that only worry madmen, and heaven is making a courtesy appearance, with the poet bouncing his sonar eye-beam off it as a ritual warm-up for the serious performance of the imagination to follow. Finally, there is no suggestion that the shapes bodied forth will be much more than pretty and delightful: the important discoveries, one feels, are going on elsewhere — (the scientist's lab in fact). But at least 'imagination' stands objective and unqualified: we must await Romanticism before it becomes 'the poet's', and finally 'my'.

This survey of poetry's magical origins has necessarily been speedy, and before we move on, a recapitulation is in order. Sympathetic magic is universally practised, both in primitive and post-primitive cultures. The arts originate in such magic. A more 'evolved' form of magic, which I have called contemplative, is that which has no other design upon its objects than their imaginative possession: philosophy, historiography, indeed most of the 'useless' arts are based on this kind of magic. It is most attractive to those who live inside the city gates and enjoy a private income; and in troubled times they will tend to revert to more useful practices such as cursing their foes and exorcizing their bad dreams. Plato's doctrine of Eternal Ideas provides the philosophic defence for the belief in contemplative magic, and those who still feel oppressed today by the declining sway of rationalist culture must find some consolation in the fact that Plato's defence has not been refuted. The reason it has not is that the relation of sameness is the ground of both sympathetic magic and rational discourse: in short, man is a magic-practising animal. Poetry since Plato has used both sympathetic and contemplative magic, but mostly the latter. When the poet can no longer assert actual identities between Man and Nature but only metaphorical resemblances, his magic is in decline. The passage from Shakespeare, which seemed at the outset of this discussion to make considerable claims for poetry, is seen to claim far less when one realizes just how much poetry *can* claim.

Yeats and Magic

It is generally said that Yeats's 'mature' verse begins with *Responsibilities*, published in 1914, and Chapter 1 of this book will begin at that point. By then he had realized that the Irish revival was not to be, and that therefore there was no question of reviving the primitive magic of the Irish bards. But some forms of word-magic were possible, and in this section I propose briefly to outline them.

As a young man Yeats was Pre-Raphaelite, *fin de siècle,* aestheticist. The credo of his early verse is clearly set forth on the first page of the *Collected Poems*:

Of old the world on dreaming fed;
Grey Truth is now her painted toy;
Yet still she turns her restless head:
But O, sick children of the world,
Of all the many changing things
In dreary dancing past us whirled,
To the cracked tune that Chronos sings,
Words alone are certain good.

In a sick world which dotes restlessly on the confections of science and materialism, the only relief is in 'songs of old earth's dreamy youth'. Words alone are certainly good because they alone can recall the human spirit from the grave in which it is buried under centuries of progress and neglect. In this poem (1889) the song is a ghostly remembering, sung in solitude: there is no suggestion that we should all link hands around the fire and sing together, thereby enclosing that public space within which the spirit might be revived, resurrected in the body politic.

That suggestion was not to come until a few years later, in the heroic plays he wrote and produced with Lady Gregory at the Abbey Theatre in Dublin. Their function was to recall 'old Eire and the ancient ways'; and though they may have done so for certain isolated minds, hands were never joined around the fire, and so the spirits remained ghostly. Yeats registers this failure in 'The Grey Rock' (1913).

In the opening years of the twentieth century a new interest in the past was awakened in Yeats. Under the very different influences of Nietzsche and Lady Gregory (and somewhat later Ezra Pound) he took up the idea of the European aristocracy, particularly the Renaissance courtier as expounded by Castiglione. The ideals of courtliness co-existed in his mind with those of 'old Eire' for a time: but this was a somewhat uneasy conjunction (as one can gather from browsing through *Responsibilities*) and in the end courtliness prevailed. During this period Lady Gregory became a mother to Yeats in certain respects and he began to think of himself as an aristocrat.

To a large extent, he traded the worship of Ancient Irish ghosts for the worship of aristocratic European ghosts; and his mind was toughened thereby. It was also rendered somewhat rigid and inflexible. But old Eire was very remote, and his attempts to contact her had been either precious and pre-Raphaelite or arcane and difficult. The aristocracy, on the other hand, was not yet quite dead — indeed, could still be found in such as Lady Gregory. By allying himself to her, he hoped to obtain direct access to a pantheon of more recently dead heroes, and to use the nourishment from such dreams to participate in contemporary Irish affairs as a last spokesman for the Protestant Ascendancy.

Thus one might characterize his 'practical' designs on the aristocracy. But his designs were also, indeed more significantly, of an 'impractical' kind, versions of contemplative word-magic; his *recherche* of the dead fathers was not only for counsel and benediction in the fight against twentieth century barbarism, but also simply for the pleasure of knowing them. These two kinds of remembrance are in no way incompatible, and Yeats frequently makes fine poetry from their interplay.

Here is an example from a late poem, 'The Statues':

> We Irish, born into that ancient sect
> But thrown upon this filthy modern tide
> And by its formless spawning fury wrecked,
> Climb to our proper dark, that we may trace
> The lineaments of a plummet-measured face.

> (CP 376)

The face referred to here is, in the first instance, Cuchulain's, the ancient Irish hero who led Pearse into the Easter Rising of 1916 (and is commemorated by a statue in the Dublin Post Office). But the poem also relates it to the faces of the statues in ancient Athens which inspired the Greeks to resist the Persian invasions. Thus Yeats's by no means parochial sense of his own dead fathers; — but more important here is the way in which their invocation is equivocal. This poem, written in 1938, states quite clearly that we Irish have, irrevocably, been wrecked. . .

None the less we climb again into the darkness of poetic memory, there to calm the fury of time present in the consolation of past integrities; perhaps to prepare once more for battle, but perhaps not.

In sum, past lineaments are worth tracing in and for themselves. The philosophic basis for this belief is in the notion of historicity, mentioned briefly on page 17 in connection with the Shakespeare passage. If the human condition and its archetypes develop through history, then it follows that life in the past was significantly other than it is now and yet 'real' in the Platonic sense: in which case we lack reality in so far as we lack access to it. That is to say, once the belief in historicity is established, the Platonist who would possess the Forms by means of contemplative word-magic must become a historian. The philosopher chiefly responsible for making this known to us was Hegel; and yet, though it commended itself immediately to the German Romantics (above all in Goethe's *Faust*), the English successfully resisted it for a long time. But not Yeats;[7] in many ways one of the last 'good Europeans', he took it in, and kept it at the heart of his poetic enterprise.

By looking at some lines from a late poem we have got ahead of our story; for in 1914 Yeats had a less extensive and sophisticated notion of whom his dead fathers were, and also a less vehement conviction of twentieth-century defeat. But defeat had even then been clearly recognized; for however he may have hoped in the first decade of the century that the aristocracy might be revived, the poems in the 1914 collection make it quite clear that he knew this could not be. The aristocrats, like the ancient Irish heroes before them, were doomed, and the best he could hope to be was their elegist. He would use his word-magic to conjure their spirits, not in order to regenerate the body politic, but only to exalt a lonely mind:

> this hand alone,
> Like some last courtier at a gypsy camping-place
> Babbling of fallen majesty, records what's gone.

(CP 138)

---

7. ' . . . no educated man will doubt that the movement of philosophy from Spinoza to Hegel is the greatest of all works of intellect' (EI 396).

These lines, written in 1913, declare the programme of the major poetry. The poet is effectively in alien country, speaking a foreign tongue; and such magic as he may produce will only mystify the gypsies seated around the fire.

The gypsies are in the first instance the Irish Catholics, from whom Yeats was drifting further and further. By 1914 he was no longer at the centre of the nationalist movement, which was becoming increasingly riven by religious and class differences. More generally, however, the gypsies represent a dispossessed European culture which had lost its settled patterns of life and become spiritually nomadic. He uses a similar image some years later:

> We shift about — all that great glory spent —
> Like some poor Arab tribesman and his tent.

(CP 276)

We shift about: Yeats, as a dispossessed European, is a nomad like the rest. But then one asks: is he not also therefore a gypsy in those earlier lines? If so, he is not easily distinguishable from the Irish Catholics, which would dismay him a good deal. Is he perhaps a gypsy dressed up as a last courtier? If so, can his record of what's gone be life-enhancing or is it only babble, and phoney babble at that? And even if he *is* a last courtier, is it sacred babble or merely babble? More generally, can one be a witch doctor or a sorcerer without an *actual* tribe believing in one's powers to raise the dead? Is not the sorcerer's magic ritually invested in tribal ceremony without which he is merely a mad man? Such questions worry the very basis of Yeats's poetry, and indeed any attempt today to make meaningful contact with the past.

In any case, by 1914 the main outlines of his poetic enterprise had emerged. The possibility of being a bard for all Ireland had gone, had indeed never really existed, and he was an isolated Anglo-Irish Protestant with aristocratic ideals in a country that was to be dominated increasingly by the Catholic petty *bourgeoisie*. What gave his poetry such a wide metaphoric range was that his Irish situation was analogous to that of western Europe about to shatter its traditional culture in the Great War. When cataclysm comes, everyone takes to the road with his tent. In certain respects Yeats joined the exodus; but as poet-mage he tried to stay behind, to haunt the shells of the burned-out houses. He resolved to summon and propitiate the departed ghosts in the hope that he might find a home amongst them, and be spared the rigours and the tedium of enforced nomadism. That he was not altogether unsuccessful in this enterprise is suggested by the confident tone in which he can assert in 'The Statues' that 'we Irish' have been wrecked in a foul tide and yet have the serenity still to contemplate past victories. Had he by 1938 solved the problem of his Irish identity? And had he found space and time in some ruined Irish tower which would allow him to climb to his proper dark for the renewal of his spirits? If so, we shall certainly find his lineaments worth tracing.

In 1975 we are still on the road. But we are also still haunted by memories of the departed ghosts — or at least memories of those memories. We look to them for consolation; and we wonder if they might not be revived. We also find that they disturb our sleep, and wonder if, through some last form of propitiation, they might not be induced to leave us alone. Yeats wondered at both these questions as well as anyone has in the twentieth century; and this makes his poetry important today, even if one's own ghosts are not Irish, nor Protestant, nor even aristocratic.

*

The kinds of magic thus far considered have usually been socially legitimized: i.e. dependent for their efficacy on a widespread belief in them throughout the society concerned. By these standards Yeats as a last courtier does not look promising as a magician. But there are esoteric as well as exoteric traditions in magic, in which the magician appears as a lonely and alienated figure, practising his art in despite of his society's disbelief. Indeed, magic in the west has largely been of this sort since institutional Christianity and modern science have dominated the thoroughfares. In the 1890s, particularly in France, poets were practising an extremely refined form of esoteric word magic called *symbolisme*. Its finest exponent was Mallarmé, and Yeats was more influenced by it than he knew. Its obvious roots are in Renaissance alchemy, but the story begins, as so many do, with Plato.

When we think about the difference between Plato's Forms and the actual objects that are instances of them, the first thing we notice is that the Forms are eternal, do not change in space and time, whereas the instances have a history, a beginning and an ending. Philosophers say that the Forms have 'being' whereas the instances are only 'becoming'. A rudimentary way of imagining this distinction is to say that the Forms are like the fixed constellations in heaven, whereas actual objects in the sub-lunary sphere, because they are a mixture of form and matter, arise out of chaos, achieve relative stability for a time, and then return to chaos. Their stability, their coherence, their perfection, their being, is measured by the degree to which their material restlessness is subdued by the shape of the constellation they seek to emulate.

From this one can see how Plato gave matter a bad name, could call the body the prison of the soul, and life a meditation on death; for the implication is that the immaterial realm has more clarity, perfection and reality than the material. This view has persisted through the ages and finds an eloquent spokesman in Shelley:

Death is the Veil which those that live call life:
They sleep, and it is lifted.

Yeats also believed it:

For wisdom is the property of the dead,
A something incompatible with life.

(CP 269)

Both of these poets make the logical 'primitive' inference from Plato's doctrine that if wisdom is immaterial and eternal, the dead know more than the living. In less primitive terms, to be wise is to be deathly.

Another way of coming to this conclusion is through the Gospel of St John. In the beginning was the Word, the *logos* of God the Father, which was made flesh in the existence of God the Son. Plato would have been appalled by the doctrine of incarnation, but relieved to find St John at least agreeing that the union of form and matter is not successful: 'He came unto his own, and his own received him not'. Where Christianity differs significantly from Platonism is in its emphasis on the flesh, and the word's failure to inform it, as witnessed in the central symbol of the crucifixion. Needless to say, the emphasis placed on the crucifixion has varied a good deal through the ages, but at present we are concerned only with what one might call the pessimistic view, the metaphysic which emphasizes the crucifixion over the incarnation, which says in effect that the word *fails* to become flesh. Such a view finds self-contradiction at the very heart of reality, asserting not only that the word cannot endure the flesh, but that its reality consists essentially in that failure; and furthermore, that the word is most essentially itself in the demonstration of its inability to endure the flesh, the climax of which is the moment of death. By this view, Christ's crucifixion is seen as the word's realization of its inalienably spiritual nature through its failure to achieve substantial union with the flesh. This kind of idealism (which may be called tragic or dialectical) received its classic exposition in the 'negative' philosophy of Hegel, who proposed it not as a typical expression of nine-teenth-century Romanticism (which it was) but as the meta-physic implicit in the Christian gospel, and therefore funda-mental to the imagination of western man.[8]

Such a philosophy is properly described as negative because it holds that nothing is but what is not; that the being of a thing is not truly achieved until the attempted union of form and matter has been undergone and negated. In Platonic terms, the Form is not finally itself until it has obscured itself in a material re-presentation, and then got free again. In Hegelian terms, spirit alienates itself into history and recovers itself by completing the knowledge of its contradic-tory nature in death. In Yeatsian terms, 'all life longs for the last day'.

The poet-magician who sees reality in this way will in general terms be concerned to re-produce this sequence in his verse. If, for example, he is involved with aristocrats, as Yeats was, he will be more concerned with their decline and fall than with their heyday, because it is only in their dying, in the recognition of their impossibility, that they achieve their true being. A fine example of this is Yeats's 'Irish Airman', and in some respects the Gregory elegy (discussed in Chapter 1). By re-presenting a significant death in poetry, the poet preserves and makes generally available the sacred

8. 'But not the life that shrinks from death and keeps itself undefiled by deva-station, but the life that endures, and preserves itself through, death is the life of the spirit. Spirit gains its truth only by finding itself in absolute dis-memberment.' (Hegel, *Phenomenology of Mind*, section 9 of the preface, Kaufmann's translation in his *Hegel*, p. 406.)

moment, an epiphany, which would otherwise have vanished. One could even argue that without his performance of last rites, the death would be unachieved, not fully comprehended; for it is only by assembling those factors which essentially require a man's death, the negation of his noblest aspirations, that we discover his true identity, the *logos* of his being; and while some men die such lucid deaths, most do not.

Mallarmé was obsessed by death and thought constantly of suicide. Its voluptous attractiveness is evident in this disturbing passage: 'Ma Beauté — dit la mort — est faite des derniers instants, lucidité, beauté, visage de ce qui serait moi sans moi — car aussitôt que je sais — (qu'on est mort) — je cesse d'être'. What is beautiful about death is the lucidity which becomes available in the last moments; a lucidity which kills off the ignorant and ugly ego and leaves only the imperishable lineaments of the true self, the *moi sans moi.* The moment this self is known, in and for itself, the search ends, and the striving ego ceases to exist.

It must now be apparent that the word 'death' in the previous paragraphs is full of metaphorical tendencies. It points not so much to the moment when a man's heart stops beating as to the moment when lucidity arrives to dispel the ignorance from which some worldly enterprise was drawing its fuel. Thus for example, Yeats's Irish Airman 'dies' when he realizes that his conventional life was obscure and confused, an impossible pursuit of unreal satisfactions. Seen in this way, a man's life may contain many 'deaths', moments of epiphany when he grasps the impossibility of what he was trying to do, and therefore tries no more. The association of ignorance with action and lucidity with inaction was central to Romanticism; and it remains central in Yeats.

The Symbolist poet may be compared to a Platonist in so far as his ultimate concern is with the spiritual forms rather than their obscured earthly instances. But since his procedure is to begin with an instance and purge it of its earthly dross, thereby revealing the form it failed to embody, he may be more obviously likened to an alchemist. His poetry is like the refiner's fire which burns away the organic impurities to reveal the golden outlines they had obscured.

The association of poetry and alchemy goes back at least to Sidney's 'Nature's world is brazen: the poets only deliver a golden': and in the 1890s, Mallarmé and Yeats were by no means the only poets who thought of themselves as alchemists.

There was no frivolous intent in this metaphor: Mallarmé, for example, believed the arts were essentially magical, and their performance a ritual in which both priest and congregation bear witness to epiphany, a deathly derivation of the sacred from the profane.

But whereas the alchemist refines lead, the poet refines language. He begins by pointing out that the relation between a word or concept and any particular instance of it (for example, the relation between 'swan' and this bird) is potentially like the relation between a Platonic Form or type and its tokens. I say potentially because ordinary linguistic operations with the word 'swan' will not of themselves evoke the ideal form since ordinary discourse obscures the type in its practical and utilitarian concern with tokens. The poet's task is to take the word, sullied by its worldly syntax, and so refine or purge it of its usual usefulness that it may grasp aspects of those objects which elude the perceptions of the man confined in ordinary language.

The aspects the poet would grasp are those which the material world refuses to entertain. He may ascribe this refusal either to a language which instrumentalizes all things, treating them as means (what they can become for me) rather than ends (what they are in themselves) or more traditionally, to the sinful nature of matter which ensures that any token will be inferior to its type. In either case he is convinced that the world as it seems is not as we know it might be, and such knowledge is what he seeks in his poetry. As Mallarmé puts it, la vraie vie est absente', and this absence is a thing's essence or Form, what it tries to be and yet is not. Just as the Freudian sees the daily drama as a masquerade sustained by the ego's ignorance and/or suppression of the id's true designs, so the Symbolist finds absence at the dynamic centre of any ongoing process; and it is this absent vitality that he would present.

Such presentation may be most easily imagined in the case of a human drama, but consider this amazing performance by Mallarmé;

Je dis: une fleur! et, hors de l'oubli où ma voix relègue aucun contour, en tant que quelque chose d'autre que les calices sus, musicalement se lève, idée même et suave, l'absente de tous bouquets.

('Crise de vers', *Variations sur un sujet)*

Here the poet's voice, by relegating the actual contours of known blossom, magically induces the essence or *idée* musically to arise, the absent source of all bouquet. Such alchemical relegation is achieved through metaphor which negates, and at the same time recalls, the perceived negativity of the world.

The presentation of absence is deathly because it obliterates or relegates or abolishes that which is normally present. It does this by making manifest what was hidden, the perfect form everything tries and fails to achieve. By publishing a thing's essential secret the poet abolishes its lively drama, which was nothing but the search for such self-discovery. When Mallarmé says 'the world exists to end in a book', he means not only that the world is abolished when it becomes book but that the book finishes what the world necessarily leaves incomplete. Poetry discovers the necessary nature of the world's incompleteness, and thereby completes it.

This is strong magic indeed. The poet or magus divines the hidden sources of life, and calls them forth. But what happens to a life which has been subjected to such violent de-mystification in the poet's verse? After such knowledge, how can one deal with tomorrow? For the sun also rises and the casual comedy returns to claim us. In short, is the poet a god who effectively brings a dead world to life, or is he some kind of demonic spider who stings at the heart and leaves only a burnt husk behind? Formulated thus abstractly, this question cannot be answered; and in the following chapters I will attempt to refine it somewhat in the light of Yeats's poetry.

Yeats's Symbolist magic was never as extreme as Mallarmé's and it is worth briefly comparing the two, particularly since this book is very much concerned with Yeats as a Symbolist poet. That Yeats was at times *symboliste*, strictly comparable to Mallarmé, can be gathered from one of his most celebrated poems, 'Byzantium'. It opens as 'The unpurged images of day recede'; and as they do so we are drawn into the alchemist's workshop where we watch the refining process as it moves a man from shade to image, 'shade more than man, more image than a shade'. Poetic knowledge, like sexual knowledge, begins in the daylight with an unpurged image of a man, and moves him through the refiner's fire:

Where blood-begotten spirits come
And all complexities of fury leave,
Dying into a dance,
An agony of trance,
An agony of flame that cannot singe a sleeve.

As the blood is abstracted, he dies, and becomes a shade. Whether the 'agony' of flame in which the death is accomplished is as harmless as the unsinged sleeve would suggest will depend on who the dancer is and how the 'golden smithies' proceed. It is, needless to say, an important question; for the poet, for the dancer, and for the readers of the poem. If, however, the death is successfully accomplished, the spirit in question has been released and made intelligible, 'more image than a shade'. The symbol of such triumph here is the golden bird, the simple perfection obscured by the blood's complexity. Once released, like Mallarmé's *fleur*, it can

               scorn aloud
In glory of changeless metal
Common bird or petal
And all complexities of mire or blood.

What makes 'Byzantium' reminiscent of Mallarmé is that it has no external subject but is a poem about the writing of poetry: the man who turns to shade and image has no name or history, but is simply 'man'. Such abstraction is the rule in Mallarmé, but very much the exception in Yeats, which is perhaps why 'Byzantium' is often found difficult or bizarre by readers of Yeats. In fact, however, if one reads it with the French in mind, it is a marvel of explicitness.

Most of Yeats's Symbolist poems, and all the ones that I shall examine in this book, name the men whose unpurged images they are seeking to refine. These men are usually Irish, and frequently dead. Yeats's interest in them arises from some blood-tie, either actual or (more frequently) metaphorical, that is to say, they are members of his extended family, and their lives bear upon his own with some gravity.

This bearing has several aspects, but the most important is the simplest: as members of his family they are parts of himself, and hence provide him with precept and example, the means of discovering who he is. As a source of personal narrative they become the more important in view of his belief (undoubtedly correct) that whereas action prospered in previous centuries, its narrative syntax was breaking down in the twentieth. This breakdown casts him appropriately enough in a sedentary trade with his eyes fixed on the past. If he can re-present their actions in his verse, he may both understand his own paralysis, and find therein some magical mitigation of it.

But when he stares at the past, the stare is returned; for if these ghosts are members of his family, so he is a member of theirs; and what they require of him in exchange for their action is his contemplation. If their function is to provide the unpurged images of day, his is to purge them in the alchemist's tower at night. Until he has done so they lack the lucidity of self-possession and cannot rest quietly, for they

> know that what disturbs our blood
> Is but its longing for the tomb.
>
> (CP 237)

'Our blood' in this context is both theirs and his, since theirs lives on in his; and its disturbance impels him to write poems in the ancestral tower. As the last of his line he is the family historian, who knows that 'Truth flourishes where the student's lamp has shone' and 'that lamp is from the tomb' (CP 207-8).[9]

In sum, his ultimate aim is exorcism; so to bring these ghosts to mind that they may cease animating his blood with either the desire or the feeling of obligation to act in the world, to take his own narrative seriously. By remembering them carefully in the alchemist's workshop he may earn the right to forget them and be forgotten by them. Having been delivered thus from history, his spirit will be 'ignorant as the dawn' (CP 164); free that is, either to be violated once again by a new historical idea or to subside utterly in the nothingness of God: 'We free ourselves from obsession that we may be nothing. The last kiss is given to the void.' [10]

9. The implication here is that when Yeats buries his family in the tomb, he becomes a ghost as well. F. H. Bradley finds a comparable ghostliness in post-Hegelian metaphysics, and is not sure he likes it: 'The shades nowhere speak without blood, and the ghosts of Metaphysic accept no substitute. They reveal themselves only to the victim whose life they have claimed, and, to converse with shadows, he himself must become a shade' (*Essays on Truth and Reality*, 1914, p. 14 footnote).
10. Letter to T. Sturge Moore, 17 April 1929.

These are extraordinary ideas, perhaps mad; and they generated extraordinary poems, as lively as any the twentieth century has seen. As with Mallarmé, there is considerable violence running through them, an alchemical violence directed at 'this pragmatical, preposterous pig of a world' (CP 268). And though there may be madness too, it is not of the frighteningly schizophrenic kind which Sartre rightly fears in Mallarmé. 'sa violence — je le dis sans ironie — est si entière et si désespérée qu'elle se change en calme idée de violence. Non, il ne fera pas sauter le monde: il le mettra entre parentèses.'[11] When the world is so preposterous that one's violence is changed into the 'calme idée de violence', one may be beyond recall, irrevocably cut off from one's real energies. Yeats was luckier than Mallarmé in never lacking specific nameable targets for his violence. The crucial factor here is that Mallarmé did not share Yeats's belief in an extended family reaching back through history and in a sense oblivious to time: hence he was stuck in the present, without narrative, and his alchemical fire had to be turned on the world as such. This probably makes his poetry more difficult both to read and to write than Yeats's, and also more contemporary: it certainly makes his violence more desperate.

*

The view which this discussion leaves us of Yeats's magic is unsettling in its strangeness. On the surface we see a last courtier, babbling of fallen majesty, telling ghost stories in an alien tongue. Gypsies around the fire find this figure foolish, and hence in certain important respects he must *be* foolish. In social or tribal terms he is neither druid nor witch doctor nor sorcerer nor priest, but by common consent only a fool, or as we say nowadays, a mad man.

But beneath the courtier's robes we see another figure, more contemporary. His arts derive from European Romanticism, the occult, alchemy and *symbolisme,* and he needs neither a thriving society nor the consent of a large and faithful congregation in order to practise. Indeed quite the reverse: his magic prospers when his society is dissolving, and its complexity is such that it could never edify more than a small

11.   Jean-Paul Sartre, Introduction to Mallarmé's *Poésies,* Paris, Gallimard, 1966, p. 5.

elect. Though he lacks the social eminence the priest enjoys in a thriving society, he claims a more potent magic; for whereas the priest as a rule merely sustains the traditional pieties, the Symbolist mage is an alchemist who finds death in life and life in death; or rather who transforms, through his word-magic, life into death, and death into life. He does this by 'knowing' his subjects in a special way, and this knowledge (as we saw in 'Byzantium') bears striking resemblances to sexual knowledge. Yeats thought of his subjects as connected to him through a kind of blood-tie; and the question that must stand behind our reading of his poetry is whether the knowledge he seeks is something sane and good or whether it is something like a fantastic version of incestuous necrophilia.

Yeats and Politics

Like most of the other major writers of his generation, such as Pound, Eliot and Lawrence Yeats has been accused of fascist political beliefs. The charge is just, but not nearly as significant as those who urge it would wish. Since I do not propose to dwell on the question of Yeats and totalitarian politics, and the subject is a touchy one, I had better say why.

Like Eliot and Pound, Yeats thought the twentieth century was a mess, and that this was so because imagination only thrives in hierarchical societies grounded in the play between aristocracy and beggary, possession and dispossession, the 'Dream of the noble and the beggar-man' (CP 369); that is to say, for a culture to prosper there must be space in which the actions of Big Men can appear, and there must also be space for the nihilist fool to put those actions in perspective. Yeats believed that such conditions had existed at various times in the past, and he praised them in his poetry.[12]

Such poetry was intended, through the techniques I have just outlined, to constitute a magical re-production of the past, and its function was to mitigate the pain of present barbarism. But like other writers of his generation, Yeats's concern with the remembrance of times past was occasionally corrupted by his desire for their return; that is to say, his contemplative word-magic was occasionally corrupted by a desire to practise black magic, a desire actually to raise the

12.   For his last word on the dialectic of noble and beggar-man, see section V of 'Under Ben Bulben' (CP 400).

dead, to bring them back to life not just to mind. I say 'corrupted' because such a desire ignores the processes of history, that aristocracy must grow like a tree, with age, in religious soil, and cannot be put together over-night. When this is attempted, the result is fascism.

Unlike Eliot and Lawrence but like Pound, Yeats had some access to the political arena, and the rather ludicrous story of his corruption has been well told in an essay by Conor Cruise O'Brien.[13] What needs emphasizing these days, however, is not his corruption but the fact that most of his poetry recognizes that the dead must stay dead, and that twentieth-century poets have no legislative powers:

> I think it better that in times like these
> A poet's mouth be silent, for in truth
> We have no gift to set a statesman right.[14]
>
> ('On Being Asked for a War Poem')

When he failed to keep this silence, which was not often, he wrote bad poetry. But when he kept it, in poems which conjured dead aristocrats in order to exorcize their ghosts, he was both seeking consolation in the past and deliverance from it through the recognition of its present impossibility. In this he was not exacerbating modern confusion but actually helping to free us from an infection which still pollutes the twentieth-century mind. As Brecht said of the dead Hitler, 'The bitch that bore him is in heat again'. Our continuing bad dreams of a Big Man to lead us are necessary to her conception of another monster; and the good magic in Yeats provides some antidote to that bad magic which still moves within us.

More relevant to a book about Yeats's poetry is the question of his historical judgements: did he not glamourize the old aristocracy and often turn a blind eye to the 'mind-forg'd manacles' by which its domination was sustained? The answer to this must be yes, and when obvious distortions of the historical record arise in the poetry (as in 'Blood and the Moon' and 'The Tower') I point them out, and try to account for them in terms of Yeats's own peculiarly uncertain social position, an insecurely middle-class Protestant in a society increasingly dominated by the catholic petty *bourgeoisie*.

13. 'Passion and Cunning', in IER.
14. In a lighter vein he makes the same point: 'So stay at home and drink your beer/And let the neighbours vote.' (CP 365).

But more generally, was his reading of history one-sided, biased in favour of the rich and against the poor? Do we not feel he took insufficient account of the labour and the suffering which were required in order to produce 'the inherited glory of the rich' (CP 225)? Once again our answer must be yes: but the assessment of such bias has more to do with values than facts, and hence it is to some extent shaped by the prevailing ideology, substantially more left-wing today than it was in Yeats's time. Bias, in short, declares one's historical situation, and Yeats's admirers must look for his in their own. But however one judges the rhetoric he made out of his quarrel with others, it is important to see that his best moments find him beyond ideology, simply getting it right:

Parnell came down the road, he said to a cheering man:
'Ireland shall get her freedom and you still break stone.'[15]

(CP 359)

---

15. The distinction I make here between rhetoric and poetry (which indeed is Yeats's own) is similar to the one outlined above (pp.14-15) between practical and contemplative magic, the former intended to influence one's neighbours, the latter intended simply to reveal the truth. Plato tried to define the difference between the two, but his attempt cannot have been completely successful, as men have been arguing about it ever since. Still, his attack on the sophists and the rhetorical skills they taught remains the best introduction to this important and difficult problem, and a lively account of it appears in Chapter 29 of Robert Pirsig's *Zen and the Art of Motorcycle Maintenance* (London, Bodley Head, 1974).

THE COURTIER-MAGE

> . . . This hand alone,
> Like some last courtier at a gypsy camping-place
> Babbling of fallen majesty, records what's gone.
>
> (CP 138)

> Versing, I shroud among the dynasties;
> quaternion on quaternion, tireless I phrase
> anything past, dead, far,
> sacred, for a barbarous place.[1]

By 1914 when *Responsibilities* was published, Yeats knew full well that neither Ireland nor any other European country was about to revive the Renaissance courtier. This knowledge did not, however, dispose him to abandon the ideals he had discovered in his Renaissance studies; indeed they appear throughout his major poetry as a yardstick by which subsequent cultures may be measured and found wanting.

But the courtly mask was by no means the only one he wore, and two of the three poems discussed in this chapter bear few traces of it. Though it frequently suited him to appear as an exiled courtier keeping old memories alive, he had other voices, both more and less contemporary. The one that particularly concerns me in this chapter is that of the Symbolist mage. Like the last courtier he is a historian who records what's gone, but instead of appearing foolish and exposed, himself going under with the old order, he seems ghostly and may be thriving on the bad news. This distinction is illustrated in the epigraphs above: the Berryman quote is thematically similar to the Yeats, but Berryman is comfortably shrouded and cheerfully versing whereas Yeats is in trouble. Because of the similarity between courtier and mage, and because Yeats often moves perplexingly from one to the other (now involved, now detached) I have called this chapter, rather awkwardly, 'The Courtier-Mage'.

The three poems in question were written between 1913 and 1918. Although they all concern contemporary Irish failures, Yeats's way of recording what's gone differs signifi-

1.   John Berryman, *Homage to Mistress Bradstreet*, London, Faber, 1959.

cantly in each case. In 'The Grey Rock' (1913) he looks back on his involvement in the fight for Irish nationalism and finds it misplaced. He proposes to retire from the Dublin stage and wander off to dream of things that cannot die because they are not tied to flesh and blood. In 'Easter 1916' he looks at a specific and heroic battle for Irish freedom and decides that it, too, was bound to fail. In the elegy for 'Major Robert Gregory' (1918) he finds in the death of an Irish aristocrat the impossibility of the courtly ideal's being realized in the twentieth century.

In each case the failure is to unite the ideal and the real, the word and the flesh, contemplation and action. The attempt to do so may be heroic, but the price may be death. Yeats is concerned not only to explore the nature of these failures but also to celebrate them as necessary, and therefore ultimately just. If he can succeed in this, he may be able to justify his own choice of 'a sedentary trade' instead of something more vigorous. On this point he is haunted by memories of a time when poets were themselves courtiers, as active as any in the realm.

What disturbs him is not only the possibility that his choice of poetry was cowardly, bloodless or insipid, but also whether as a poet his interest in the deaths of others is not somewhat ghoulish As Symbolist mage he buries his fellows, confers on them the gift of intelligible death. But how does he live? Is he some kind of nihilist, finding in other people's passion and pain the evasion of his own humanity? Or is he a priest who has sacrificed his own part in the play in order to provide rites of passage for his fellows, to conduct them across that difficult river that separates life from death? This is another way of formulating the problem, mentioned in the Introduction (p. 29), of the 'agony' which alchemy involves; the following discussion should bring it into focus.

'The Grey Rock' (1913)

The period 1903-13 was full of shocks and disillusionments for Yeats. Maud Gonne married in 1903. In the public realm there was the *Playboy* fiasco, the dispute over Lane's pictures, Lutyens's gallery, the Abbey troubles and the attacks on Yeats in the Dublin press. Moore mocked him in *Ave*, and then Synge died in 1909 and Pollexfen seventeen months later. During most of this time Yeats was working at the Abbey Theatre, writing strange implausible plays and little verse. Some idea of his depressed state of mind can be gathered from the diary extracts of 1909 published in the *Autobiographies*. As his disenchantment with the Irish grew, so did his unpopularity; and his estrangement is nicely symbolized in his acceptance of a British Civil List pension in 1910, for which he was dubbed 'pensioner Yeats'. In sum, by the time he began writing 'The Grey Rock', not only did he know that he was not to lead the Irish revival, but he had been isolated as an unreliable Protestant in the pay of the English.

This situation lends considerable irony to his setting the poem in Celtic Ireland. Whereas 'To a Wealthy Man' (written three months earlier) quite openly reproaches Dublin for not having read Castiglione, here Yeats digs himself into ancient ground which his enemies would claim more theirs than his. Strategically it was a shrewd move, and indeed the defence he mounts is so clever that it is rarely noticed, the poem often being taken simply as a Pre-Raphaelite tale in memory of his old friends Johnson and Dowson. But to do this is to underestimate both the italicized remarks which interrupt the tale, and the fact that 'The Grey Rock' opens a collection of poems in which the first six are concerned with denouncing the Irish philistines.

At the simplest level Yeats is addressing the question of whether his thoughts and activities over the previous years were either unpatriotic or irrelevant. As a Pre-Raphaelite wanderer he had spent some time with Fergus in the woods listening to 'lover's music'; and he obviously does not intend to apologize for that. But as a reader of Castiglione and a public figure he had also been attracted by the prospect of sword-play on the Dublin stage, and he is wondering if this was not perhaps misguided or at least mistimed. The question of timing is central, and it is ingeniously handled here by the rather cinematic technique of inter-cutting the ancient narrative with contemporary comments, which effectively suggest that energies which look heroic in a ninth-century landscape do not easily translate to the present.

The story tells of the passion conceived by the goddess Aoife for a young Irish warrior. In return for his love she promises him immortality in the form of invisibility on the battlefield. He accepts, easily dispatches some Danes, decides he is cheating, renounces the goddess, becomes visible again, and is killed. Aoife is annoyed, and asks her fellow immortals, assembled in solemn and drunken conclave, to harry the dead man's sleep; but for reply they only empty their wine cups on her. Baptized back into her proper society, she remembers that whereas sexuality is for humans, gods get off on their indifference.

The gods find wisdom in their wine. They understand the human drama, how its excitement depends on its dangerousness, but the price of such wisdom is detachment. As ghostly witnesses to the round of mortality, its folly and its sublimity, they may be appropriate patrons for the kind of poetry Yeats writes. The warrior, on the other hand, is a patriot son of Ireland: nonchalant in the face of death (the supreme courtly virtue for Yeats) he answers his country's call and plays by the rules. Yeats, though similarly tempted to join in the battle for Dublin's soul, claims he has 'kept faith' to the goddess Aoife. Although he obviously *did* join in to some extent, we can accept his statement, for his battle never really got past the planning stage. What he is suggesting is that had it done so he too would have had to forsake the wandering Aoife, become a visible man, and die into Dublin's confusion.

The warrior's refusal of Aoife's divine protection can be seen as both genuinely heroic and rather stupid, even weak. On the one hand a man of action can do no better than risk his life in the defence of Mother Ireland, and honour requires that he shun the corrupting favours of a decadent and bibulous faery queen. On the other hand, the ironic immortals (and their loyal servants the poets) are not unduly impressed by the warrior's death wish, or as Fergus puts it, the 'foolish labourer who wastes his blood to be another's dream' (CP 37). The ambiguity then, is that 'God possesses the heavens — but He covets the world' (M 13), and both poets and faery queens occasionally envy the heroic follies of which the non-ironic passionate man is capable: 'It is hard to give up those generalizations [such as *pro patria mori*] through which the will flings itself upon the world, those gleams of future victory, that are to one as though one cried aloud, all that makes one for the moment, of the race of the eagles.' [2] In short, the warrior *does* represent virtues Yeats admires and indeed regrets in himself — in the previous poem for example,

2. From Yeats's diary in 1910, cited in Jeffares's *W. B. Yeats: Man and Poet*, p.163.

among the 'old fathers' whose pardon he is seeking are 'soldiers that gave, whatever die was cast'. But one cannot be both soldier *and* wandering poet, and Yeats clearly thinks the latter calling preferable, particularly in present times when there are so few causes worth dying for and so few noble warriors worth dying with.

In this connection one can see in the warrior's death a moral for Maud and the sisters Gore-Booth, all three of whom Yeats frequently reproached for treacherously sacrificing beauty in order to give loud service to the cause of Irish nationalism and left-wing politics.[3] These three got their timing wrong, did not realize that theirs was not an age of noble battles, and hence instead of a warrior's death they were rewarded (if one is to believe Yeats) with noisy minds and a general coarsening of the features:

> For arrogance and hatred are the wares
> Peddled in the thoroughfares.
>
> (CP 214)

When one remembers that Yeats had been in love with at least one of them,[4] one can see a parallel between him and the rejected Aoife. But in Aoife's place he has mixed feelings about their departure from his life, and one can find both malice and dutch courage in his lonely triumph at the end of the tale as he

> with Goban's wine adrip,
> No more remembering what had been,
> Stared at the gods with laughing lip.[5]

3. See CP 263.

4. Maud and perhaps Eva. See Torchiana, pp. 185-6.

5. The reader may object that since this poem mentions neither Maud nor the Gore-Booths, I should not bring them into a discussion already quite rich enough in allusiveness. My reply is that they belong here because this is the period in which they 'betrayed' Yeats, they were significant figures in his Irish drama, and we can assume they were on his mind, perhaps too painfully to be named at this time. (The poems which *do* name their 'betrayal' were not written until several years later. CP 211 and 263.)

Dowson and Johnson are difficult to place in the allegory, for they stand somewhere between the gods and the warrior. As poets they were in some way bound to the immortals, but since their contract with the Muse required them to act out a form of gradual suicide ('t'was wine or women or some curse') they end up with the warrior as worldly actors not divine spectators. Like the gods they drunk wine, but it was of a different sort:

> And though at bottling of your wine
> Old wholesome Goban had no say.

In sum, the poets of the tragic generation served another Muse, less wholesome than Aoife, but less cold.

This reading of the poem has now become quite complicated. Aoife is both the muse to whom Yeats has kept faith, and she is also the poet Yeats who has been betrayed by the warriors of Irish nationalism, Maud Gonne above all. In both cases the moral is that even though poets may envy the heroics of politics and the tempting 'folly of a fight with a common wrong or right' (CP 264) their sacrifice to the muse may be the nobler one, at least in the present age when common fights are so *common.* But the sacrifice they make is quite costly; for wandering poets lack both social connection and the enduring love of a woman; and since serving Aoife does not altogether warm the blood, one may have recourse either to wine (Johnson) or harlots (Dowson) or both. Yeats had recourse to neither, and whether he envied his friends' unwholesome fall into the flesh, or disapproved, or saw it as a legitimate path he did not take, or thought a similar fate might ultimately claim him, is a question this poem raises and does not answer.

At the end of 'The Grey Rock' in any case he stands with Aoife, restored after a brief dalliance with earthly engagements to his proper indifference, on stony ground. He had tried to be Ireland's lover, to bestow immortality upon her, and above all on one of her daughters, but she treacherously refused the gift; and now that his mind is right he will cleave to the laughing lip:

> . . . and I choose the laughing lip
> That shall not turn from laughing, whatever rise or fall;

The heart that grows no bitterer although betrayed by all;
The hand that loves to scatter, the life like a gambler's
throw.

(CPL 243)

Placed at the opening of the 1914 collection this poem casts
an ironic eye on the epigraph 'In dreams begins responsibility',
informing the reader that this much misconstrued phrase is by
no means announcing that henceforth Yeats will stop fooling
around and become a serious citizen. His version of respon-
sibility is much more complex than that. He will offer his
mind and poetry as a kind of no man's land where eternity
may explore the ways it falls in love with the productions of
time, and vice versa.

'Easter 1916'

As a comment upon a political event this poem is a master-
piece of cunning and tact; for however shallow one's grasp of
Yeats's politics, one cannot but see that this event (which
found him, appropriately enough, visiting Sir William Rothen-
stein in Gloucestershire) must have perplexed him deeply.
On the one hand, his early labours with Maud and the others
for Ireland's freedom doubtless disposed him to sympathize
with any gesture, however futile or ill-advised, against the
English tyranny; and as Hone points out, 'his English friends
noticed that at last he seemed to be moved by a public event'
(WBY 299). On the other hand, this was a new generation
of patriots, who may have thought that Yeats was a name to
conjure with on certain occasions, but this was not one of
them; and hence Yeats 'fretted somewhat that he had not
been consulted' (WBY 300).

Even more disturbing for Yeats was the fact that most of
these men were disreputably extreme, Catholic, and petty
bourgeois;[6] indeed many of them were victims of that ill-
informed hatred he had been denouncing for years from his
towering loneliness:

The root of it all is that the political class in Ireland — the
lower-middle class from whom the patriotic associations
have drawn their journalists and their leaders for the last

6. Connelly was a communist.

ten years — have suffered through the cultivation of hatred as the one energy of their movement, a deprivation which is the intellectual equivalent to a certain surgical operation. Hence the shrillness of their voices. [1909]

(A 486)

Finally, viewed as drama, the Rising itself was more like farce than tragedy, a parody of Blake's Orc arising and breaking the shackles of empire.[7] And yet despite all these reservations and indeed because of some of them, this was a public event which moved Yeats and to which he felt impelled to respond. The staggering problem was how to do so without sounding either mean or envious, and above all without compromising the principles about history and hatred and culture and heroism which he had been elaborating over the years.

His perplexities are aptly registered at the outset in the contrast between 'vivid faces' and the Georgian grey — an elegant grey of settled sobriety that mocks and in turn is mocked by present vividness, which finds it faded. Amidst such ambiguity simple narrative is difficult, and Yeats proceeds hesitantly and obliquely through the first two sections, as if uncertain where the meanings lie, what myth could draw the strands together. The over-all impression is of the poet puzzling an event which he had not foretold, in which he played no part, and yet whose world-historical significance was such as to have transformed utterly some of Ireland's base and debased metals into something rich and strange.

But though the first two sections do suggest that this is a poem about an event which took place somewhere else, a careful reading of the last two sections discloses the Symbolist poet finding in an external event a complex symbol through which he can explore his own poetic processes. The modulation which leads us from history into the poet's mind is supremely managed, so that one feels no coercion, no palpable designs in the poet's voice as it moves from 'they and I but lived' through 'our part but to murmur' to 'I write it out in a

7. O'Casey presents it as farce in *The Plough and the Stars,* and he should know. Not unlike Yeats in this poem, he can register its gravity only on the lips of the mother who murmurs the names of the dead. For O'Casey's Catholic sensibility, this gesture of *pieta* is sufficient, and in *Juno and the Paycock* is very moving. To the protestant Yeats, however, the voice of Mother Ireland not come easily, and hence he must try to make the men heroic after all — an extraordinarily difficult task, and the wonder is that he succeeds as well as he does.

verse'. The movement from history to mind, from them to him, is accomplished by suggesting that their sacrifice is analogous to the one he makes daily in order to serve his Muse. The only point at which his poise is threatened is in the last section where he briefly interrupts the analogical process and returns to the event;

What is it but nightfall?
No no, not night but death.

The destructive potential of this line not only for this poem but for the whole of Yeats's poetic idealism can scarcely be overestimated; for in it he is considering that death may not be a metaphor for poetry, that its sting may be incorrigibly other, not susceptible of poetic mediation; which is of course unthinkable, and so after a couple of lines on the politics of martyrdom, Yeats returns to familiar ground:

enough
To know they dreamed and are dead.

Enough, that is, to see them, like myself, as victims of the dream; for as such, they lie within my ken, and I may encompass them. To view them predominantly from 'the outside', as men who acted politically and were annihilated by the English, would bring to light among other things the fact that they acted and are dead and I did not and am alive; and hence I should have to write a different poem, whose metaphors would resist my penetration, and which would have to deal with such alien questions as the political implications of the rising.

All things considered, the poem is probably enriched by this apparently rambling and uncertain sequence in the final section, not only because it indicates that the poet may be troubled by thoughts of the impropriety of appropriating other men's deaths, but also because it shows him aware of the difficulties of writing a poem which 'holds in a single thought reality and justice' (AV 25); in this case, the reality of their dying and the justice of his metaphors. Whether or not one finds that he has succeeded in holding death and sleep in a single thought, one should admire the probity which led him at least to recognize the problem.

On the other hand, the fact that the problem arises at all, that Yeats is writing poetry which to some extent attempts to smother death with metaphor, is bound to make the reader uneasy, particularly in an age increasingly anxious about its ability to register death's sting with gravity. In the end, the extent of one's unease depends largely on how one views Yeats's attempt to identify with the insurgents through the image of the stone, and to admit that in his own way he is as bewildered as they. To my mind this identification is supremely well executed; and if it does not altogether dispose of the problem, it at least renders the situation sufficiently complex and ambiguous to silence any categorical reproach.

At the simplest level, the stone of moral and political fanaticism troubles the living stream because it is necessarily insensitive to the 'minute particulars of mankind', which are endlessly various and constantly changing, and which alone can 'silence the mind' (CP 193). Yeats acquired his reverence for Minute Particulars from Blake:

> He who would do good to another must do it in Minute
> Particulars:
> General Good is the plea of the scoundrel, hypocrite and
> flatterer,
> For Art and Science cannot exist but in minutely
> organized Particulars
> And not in generalizing Demonstrations of the Rational
> Power.
> (B 503)

Thus Blake answers Rousseau, and by implication all exponents of such political abstractions as 'the general good'. The stony vacancy of such inert categories, and the life-denying sacrifices men make to them, threaten life's delicate integrities in such a way that eventually one may find 'every Minute Particular harden'd into grains of sand' (B 471). Blake would have us remember that the body politic is composed of living bodies whose needs and subtleties require loving attention:

> Labour well the Minute Particulars, attend to the
> Little-ones,
> And those who are in misery cannot remain so long
> If we but do our duty: labour well the teeming Earth. (B 503)

It is as if Yeats were thinking of this passage when he says

>   our part
> To murmur name upon name,
> As a mother names her child . . .

Thus in Blake's terms, the insurgents became bewildered by forgetting that life resides in the minute; and this surely is the implication of the poem's third section, in which 'minute' occurs six times. By ignoring 'the Little-ones', the insurgents themselves became childish; and their deaths might even be seen as life's rejection of their abstraction — (for the poem makes no mention of the English executioners):

> And what if excess of love [and hate]
> Bewildered them till they died? [8]

On the other hand, the singleness of their vision, their reckless and unswerving commitment to an ideal Ireland that never could be, *was* heroic, and despite their bewilderment it may qualify them to dine at journey's end with O'Leary and the other colonizers of Romantic Ireland. Indeed, when Yeats writes out their names in a verse, he is in effect making it so — providing patronymics for men who up until then were nameless, below the salt.

Though the stream's surface appears to hold a mirror up to nature, thereby containing the endless variety, this mirror is broken by the intrusion of horse and rider, a Heraclitean horseman happening to remind us that one cannot step twice into the same river. The only possibility for permanence lies in the stone: sitting always on the bottom, it may be eternally present as it never moves.

But the stone represents superhuman stillness, a permanence denied to all men except perhaps such ghostly poets as Yeats; for when an active man becomes enchanted by such an ideal, his horse will trouble the living stream in a much more damaging way than the pious plashing of the Irish rider.

(CP 305)

---

8. Cf. 'Such love and hatred seek no mortal thing but their own infinity, and such love and hatred soon become love and hatred of the idea' (EI 181).

The difference between the stone and the heart it enchants is that whereas the latter troubles the stream, the former simply outlines and preserves it. The stone of 'The Statues' charts a middle course between these two, coercing no one and yet providing still forms to animate reverie (which in turn puts down the 'many-headed'). The crucial difference between the statues and the Easter stone is the latter's simplicity, inarticulacy, even emptiness; and one could argue that this structural difference is responsible for their inspiring such different sorts of dream.

Whereas the statues proclaim the measurement that began our might and provide a bridge from ideal to real, the stone is the talisman of an altogether more decadent, desperate, even nihilistic age. At its most passive, as in 'Tom the Lunatic', it evokes the witnessing eyeball of a Berkleyian Idealism, in the midst of all, certainly, but capable only of recording the cyclical rhythms of nature. When it enters the minds of active men, however, like the philosophers' stone it can bewilder them with dreams of excessive love and hatred.

Yeats the poet knows something of sacrifice and the stony heart, and indeed something of the clown's heroic bewilderment; hence, although he works in a different theatre, he can sing both knowingly and sympathetically of the sixteen dead whose peer in some sense he is. Because the poet acts through words of course, he lives on to tell the tale, but in the end it may be his as much as theirs. Another way of putting it is in the terms of mother and child. As the ecumenical voice of Mother Ireland, Yeats is concerned to

Murmur name upon name,
As a mother names her child
When sleep at last has come
On limbs that had run wild.

The child on this reading is also Yeats, who, like the others, is dead to the world through having sacrificed himself to the service of the ideal in a tragic age. The difference is that he can redeem his own sacrifice through poetry, namely by recognizing and accepting it, whereas theirs, unless the Mother of God can hear them, must wait upon his healing touch.[9]

9. The fact that Easter is a time when a stone is rolled away and a man arises, and through his resurrection other dead men are redeemed, is a coincidence which furnishes an allusive potential of considerable richness; but since Yeats had the

'In Memory of Major Robert Gregory' (1918)

In Chapter 2 of his *Romantic Image* Professor Kermode persuasively suggests that Yeats's search for an elegiac voice on this occasion took him to the Renaissance, and specifically to Cowley's 'Ode on the Death of Mr. William Harvey' (RI 38-40). Robert Gregory, 'our Sidney and our perfect man', displayed the Unity of Being of which the Renaissance courtier is the archetype, and Yeats is here concerned with both recording what's gone and defining his relationship to it. The poem is clearly a distinguished one, but to my mind more for the uneasiness and uncertainties it almost conceals than for the complexity it almost masters.

The first two stanzas ingeniously locate the poetic space through which the meditation moves, that quintessentially Yeatsian middle ground from which an eye both cold and not so cold is cast upon the dialectics of life and death, action and contemplation, courtiers and artists, becoming and being. Just as the occasion for this timeless meditation which will climb the winding stair into darkness is a supper party that never was, so the language is both vernacular and highly formalized. The tableau is lively, full of domestic detail, and yet also utterly empty, 'for all that come into my mind are dead'. Indeed 'we're almost settled in our house', our end and our beginning, but not quite.[10]

The last line of the second stanza picks up the last line of the first and together they arouse in the reader the suspicion that perhaps what is also on the poet's mind is the possibility that he too is dead, or at least deathly — which raises the possibility that only dead things come to my mind, or even that bringing things to mind is somehow a deadening act. This suspicion is borne out by the next three stanzas in which he identifies in turn ('a portion of my mind and life') with three dead friends whose lives were also pale and shadowy. But not *simply* pale and shadowy; the important point about all three is the problematic, indeed ultimately impenetrable expression they gave to the tension between action and

---

good taste not to insist upon it, I think we should not either. As well as Christ, of course, the terrible beauty calls forth a slouching beast, that beast which makes an objective mess of twentieth-century politics and forces subjective men to write Symbolist poems.

10. This is the first of several tower poems in which Yeats entertains the ghosts of absent friends. Others are 'Meditations in Time of Civil War', 'Dialogue of Self and Soul', 'Blood and the Moon', 'The Tower', 'The Black Tower'.

contemplation. Thus they have been summoned to the winding stair not as three men who simply chose the *vita contemplativa* over the *vita activa*, but as three good reasons for not making facile generalizations about the two kinds of perfection between which the intellect of man is forced to choose.

Lionel Johnson clearly fascinated Yeats as a man who half-desired the world he had renounced and which gradually reclaimed him in such an undignified fashion. Not only was he capable of brooding on sanctity while falling into a stupor,[11] but could spend much time carousing with Dowson whose life was 'a sordid round of drink and cheap harlots' (EI 492) and still manage to exclaim, 'I wish those people who deny the eternity of punishment could realize their unspeakable vulgarity' (A 223). He was both 'contemptuous of all that we call human life' (A 223) and yet

in some half-conscious part of him desired the world he had renounced. I was often puzzled as to when and where he could have met the famous men or beautiful women whose conversation, often wise, and always appropriate, he quoted so often, and it was not till a little before his death that I discovered these conversations were imaginary.(A 305)

Synge, who was 'timid, too shy for general conversation' (A 345) was urged by Yeats to the Aran islands because 'I felt he needed something to take him out of his morbidity and melancholy' (A 343). There he found a life which he could not share but from which he could fashion, with the extraordinary intensity of the dying artist, a lively vision which redeemed the fruitless years of his wandering.

Pollexfen, the least complex of the three, gave up what little life he had as a young man, and found some justification for doing so, as well as some resolution of his pervasive melancholy, in the abstract certainties of the astrologer.[12] Thus all three, though in quite different ways, were estranged from society and the active life, unaccommodated men who sought in the solitude of imagination some form of communion which the world could not provide. Yeats is 'accustomed to their lack of breath' not only because they are dead, but because even in life their faces (like his own) were somewhat

11.   See A 223 and A 318-19.
12.   A 69-71 and A 255-70.

breathless — which I take to be not so much a reproach as an indication of possible saintliness:

> A mouth that has no moisture and no breath
> Breathless mouths may summon.[13]

(CP 280)

It is at this point that Gregory's death is introduced, smoothly enough it may seem, and yet to my mind it is an event which the rest of the poem tries unsuccessfully to assimilate and from which it does not recover. The key phrase in the sixth stanza is 'that discourtesy of death'. The poet and the three shades are normally breathless:

> What portion in the world can the artist have
> Who has awakened from the common dream
> But dissipation and despair?

(CP 182)

In other words, artist-contemplatives in the present age are claimed by death before they die, and can only manifest themselves in the physical world as melancholy, dissipated, timid and sluggish. The courtier on the other hand has no business but *nonchalance,* which involves among other things a childlike ignorance of death; or rather, the courtier's wilful recklessness, though in one sense a courting of death, is in another sense a refusal to take it seriously; and thus when it is met, there can be no question of either reverence or deference: 'Horseman, pass by!' The courtier-poet is obliged to notice the reckless passing of his fellows with an answering nonchalance of the hand, and Yeats discharges this obligation magnificently in 'An Irish Airman'. If in the elegy he seems to stumble in the sixth stanza and finally cries out in pain at the end, then we are forced to suppose that this poem is at least to some extent the work of a modern hand, a twentieth-century man,

> Timid, entangled, empty and abashed,
> Lacking the countenance of our friends.   (CP 180)

13.   'Breathless' is like the dawn in its duality, referring both to the moment of intense life from which epiphanies may break and also to the ghostly condition, neither dead nor alive, which Yeats calls the 'death-in-life'. Cf. also the Irish Airman, who chooses not to 'waste his breath' on life, unlike those grey men who 'breathed on the world with timid breath' (CP 108).

And indeed we knew this right from the start. The friends that cannot sup with us and thereby constitute our ghostly identity are not a band of dashing cavaliers — 'Aye, horsemen for companions'—(CP 108), but rather three examples of the 'gentle, sensitive mind' as the result of which we modern men 'have lost the old nonchalance of the hand' (CP 180).[14] Without this nonchalance, and even though we are accustomed to a lack of breath, we find it extremely difficult to deal with a man like Robert Gregory; for we can neither admit him to our ghostly company of contemplatives nor register his passing as a mere discourtesy. Thus the difficulty of accepting Gregory's death arises neither because he was a courtier nor because he was a modern artist, but because he was capable of being both.

His death is not simply a discourtesy because he was not simply a Renaissance courtier but a complex twentieth-century man, a possible initiate of our secret discipline. Hence it is not sufficient to send him off with a long blast upon the hunting horn; and so I have assembled my artist friends to see if we can find some more 'appropriate commentary'. On the other hand he does not appear to be one of us, for in the ninth stanza he seems to have overcome the dissociation of sensibility which has crippled each one of us. And this is painful indeed; for if he could have been both courtier *and* artist, in the twentieth century, then he moves outside our antinomies and reveals their inadequacy. We are then no longer the tragic victims of an 'objective', 'critical' age in which action and contemplation are necessarily in conflict, but merely some few of Nietzsche's 'bungled and botched' for whom there is no world-historical apology; which is of course unthinkable, and hence the Major is rather deliberately killed off in the eleventh stanza. That is to say, his death cannot be seen as an accident which needlessly deprives us of our perfect man but rather (though this is not apparent without considerable exegesis) he is forced to choose death as the only way of preserving his perfections from the erosions of time.

The theological necessity for this execution is provided throughout *A Vision* but more particularly perhaps in the following passage:

14.   The fact that Pollexfen was a horseman in his muscular youth only increases the painful irony which separates us from the unified beings.

[Dowson and Johnson] had taught me that violent energy, which is like a fire of straw, consumes in a few minutes the nervous vitality, and is useless in the arts. Our fire must burn slowly, and we must constantly turn away to think, constantly analyse what we have done, be content even to have little life outside our work, to show, perhaps, to other men, as little as the watch-mender shows, his magnifying-glass caught in his screwed-up eye. Only then do we learn to conserve our vitality, to keep our mind enough under control and to make our technique sufficiently flexible for expression of the emotions of life as they arise.

(A 318)

Thus Gregory only *seemed* to have sufficiently unified being to combine horsemanship and the secret discipline in the twentieth-century. He knew that the price of life was a choice between perfection of the life or of the work, and he decided that the price was too high. That as a matter of fact Yeats thought of Gregory as having chosen death as an escape from the unattractive alternatives of aristocratic inconsequentiality on the one hand and the suppressed energies of the artist on the other is persuasively argued by Kermode in the second chapter of his *Romantic Image*.

The final line of the eleventh stanza comes across as a sigh of relief. While it would be perverse to suggest at this point that Yeats was pleased by Gregory's death, it is rather different to suggest that he may have been relieved at having resolved the challenge, indeed the threat, posed by the Gregory of stanzas 7-10 to the company assembled in the tower.

And yet *has* he resolved it? When we look at Gregory's death in the eleventh stanza, we find the image of his ecstatic flame-out is a curious one: instead of self-immolation as the final gesture of the hero — a hero who knew he could not continue to be an aristocrat and keep his intensity (such as we might have in 'The Irish Airman Foresees his Death') — we find a figure who looks more like one of Yeats's adored alchemists, 'turning lead into gold, weariness into ecstacy, bodies into souls, the darkness into God' (M 270). In short, the idea of consuming the entire world in one small room (are we not in the tower?) looks very like the self-annihilation achieved by the (usually

German) alchemist-philosopher's appropriation of, and identity with, the totality of created forms.

At this point it must occur to the reader that the poem is out of control, for the gap separating the tenth and eleventh stanzas is radical, unbridgeable. The man who dies in the eleventh stanza may have a certain amount in common with the Irish airman but he bears little resemblance to the courtier described in the previous four stanzas. In what follows I shall attempt to account for this anomaly, as a rule trusting the tale not the teller, the aim being to arrive at a reading of the poem which incorporates the strangeness of the eleventh stanza as one of its principal meanings.

The uneasiness one detects in this stanza is borne out in the poem's conclusion, where Yeats seems to be dallying with the Romantic-Symbolist practice of writing poems which explore the conditions of their own impossibility. [15] He says that what he *had* intended to do was to summon all those friends who have made him what he is ('friendship is all the house I have' [A 478]) and register their particular portions of his mind and life, and then construct a unifying myth, a 'fable of identity' which would compose the disparities and make them all fit into the tower. This activity seemed to be nicely under way until the ghost of Robert Gregory came knocking at the gate in the sixth stanza. As we have seen, he proved difficult to accommodate; indeed, if we take the conclusion seriously, impossible; for it implies that the thought of Gregory's death defied expression, could not be made intelligible. In other words, the eleventh stanza, in which the attempt is made, is here recognized as a failure, an inarticulacy which does not achieve the solidity of speech.

A tough-minded reader may object that this interpretation is becoming needlessly complex, and that the conclusion simply means that no amount of words and *explication* can soothe the pain of a bitter loss; in other words the poem is admitting its incapacity to deal with (that is, incorporate and master) the absurdities of life and death. While this is immediately plausible, and may even have been the poet's conscious intention, it is only part of the story; for not only would such an admission be uncharacteristic of Yeats at this point in his career, but such a reading ignores many of the

15. The philosophical origin of this practice is in Hegel, and a stimulating discussion of it can be found in chapter 5 of Erich Heller's *The Artist's Journey into the Interior*.

tale's complexities. While it is I think correct to infer that the poet is unsatisfied by the account he has given of Gregory's death, it is surely evident from the poem that what is troubling the poet is not simply an existential grief to which art cannot minister. It is something which, to Yeats at any rate, is rather more important and certainly more complex than that.

At the end of the poem the ghost of Robert Gregory is still shaking the shutter; that is, still seeking admission to the poet's mind and tower, and yet still mocking it from without. [16] Like other ghosts in Yeats's mythologies, he is not sleeping soundly in the tomb because his being has not yet been digested and refined in the purgatorial fires of poetry. [17] He remains 'other', moving outside the tower's antinomies. Yeats is vitally interested in providing this kind of purgatorial intelligibility, not only because without it the ghosts remain homeless, but also because their home is his home, namely, the tower, his mind, God's mind; and if they stay outside, like disobedient children, they threaten and mock his vast ambitions. ·

In what sense then does Gregory elude the poet's grasp? First, like the swans in the preceding poem, he provides an image of unified being which mocks the poet's shadowy state. In life, as we have noted, he was both poet and courtier, and since this is unthinkable, his death had to be construed as a recognition of this unthinkability; that is to say, having incarnated superhuman qualities he had to be returned to the godhead or else chaos is come again.

But there is another problem, more personal. Yeats had simply *envied* Gregory's effortless mastery in realms active and contemplative for a long time (C 163). This envy was made the more vivid by the fact that Yeats was competing with this man for Lady Gregory's maternal blessing — indeed Yeats had become his own 'dear friend's dear son' by adoption. [18] In view of this, some reference to Abel and Cain is not irrelevant; and as a result one finds more complex energies in the line 'What made us dream that he could comb grey hair?'

16.   Cf.   *The ghost of Roger Casement*
              Is beating on the door.
                        (CP 352)

17.   Cf. 'Crazy Jane and Jack the Journeyman', 'Byzantium', *Purgatory* and the parts of *A Vision* which deal with 'the dreaming back'.

18.   'I am only doing for him' [Lady Gregory] added, 'what I would do for my son. I feel for him as if he were my son' (WBY 165).

If this point is taken, it puts us in a position to offer (though in a tentative voice) some explanation of the curious imagery of the eleventh stanza. Yeats approaches the execution with trepidation not only because he knows it will be difficult, but also because he has some perception, however faint, of the impropriety of his undertaking. As a result he offers Gregory the noblest death he can imagine; that is to say, he attempts to cast him if not in his own image then in the image of the alchemists he so admired. This gesture, though confused at one level, makes sense in the context of brotherly love-hate suggested above. But Gregory refuses the gesture, refuses to wear the death mask Yeats provides, refuses to 'lie down and die'; and because Yeats realizes this, the poem ends where it began, with the ghost of Gregory still outside:

> I had thought, seeing how bitter is that wind
> That shakes the shutter, to have brought to mind
> All those that manhood tried, or childhood loved
> Or boyish intellect approved,
> With some appropriate commentary on each;
> Until imagination brought
> A fitter welcome; but a thought
> Of that late death took all my heart for speech.

Postscript on Kermode's Reading of 'An Irish Airman' and 'In Memory of Major Robert Gregory'

In the second chapter of his *Romantic Image*, Frank Kermode presents readings of these two poems which differ significantly from mine. Since I am substantially indebted to the *Romantic Image*, it seems appropriate to engage his arguments in some detail.

Our differences over 'An Irish Airman' are significant but not radical. Kermode suggests that we should see the airman as a Romantic artist-contemplative who finds in death a resolution (or is it evasion?) of the tragic conflict which forces man to choose between perfection of the life and of the work. To support his case he provides convincing evidence that Yeats in fact thought of Robert Gregory's death in these terms.

The objection to this reading is that it interpolates meanings into a poem which stands very well (indeed rather better) without them. This poem is entitled '*An* Irish Airman . . .', and it nowhere suggests that he was an artist, far less that he was labouring under the mythic weight of Romantic Alienation.

Kermode's procrustean designs on the poem are evident in the gloss he provides on 'A lonely impulse of delight': 'The impulse is from within; it is an impulse to resolve the tension between the growing absorption of the dream and the desire for society and the pleasures of action' (RI 37). If one consults the ten lines which precede the 'lonely impulse', one finds nothing to corroborate Kermode's statement: no suggesttion of a dreaming artist, nor of a man desiring social connection, and certainly not of a man perplexed by the conflict between the two. All we find, and surely it is enough, is that the airman has none of the desires and expectations which traditionally (or perhaps one should say 'conventionally') drive warriors into battle.

Dicing elegantly with life and death in the absence of meaningful social connection is neither a very recent nor a particularly esoteric discovery in the history of human play: Russian roulette in one form or another has been around for some time. And although the game forced upon the alienated artist may be construed in these terms, there is nothing in the terms of this poem to suggest the alienated artist. In short, by reading 'alienated artist' for 'Irish airman' Kermode constricts the poem's range, and needlessly complicates an image which to my mind Yeats is at pains to keep extended in a 'low definition'.

Indeed, the main drawback to Kermode's reading is that it obscures the poem's admirably *simple* and *universal* narrative line; that is, the sense in which it is saying 'Once upon a time there was a young man from Kiltartan'. Whereas the elegy is concerned with a possible initiate of 'our secret discipline', this poem comes out of Kiltartan Cross and follows a man exchanging (what seem to him) the meaningless ties of historical situation for the freedoms of a playfulness beyond good and evil, in which the usual distinctions between life and death are dissolved. It is a marvellous story, and Yeats has carefully kept out of it any details which would limit its accessibility to those who feel qualified to identify with Robert Gregory, Ireland's artist-aristocrat. It seems to me a remarkably democratic gesture from a poet to whom such generosity did not come easily.

*

In his reading of 'In Memory of Major Robert Gregory' Kermode again sees Gregory primarily as an artist oppressed by the conflict between action and contemplation:

> I speak as though Gregory were treated in this poem as an artist-contemplative and as nothing else; and this is almost true.
> . . . the exploration of the significance of Gregory's death as the artist's escape . . . is the main theme of the elegy. Apart from the stanza about Gregory's foolhardy horsemanship, the poem treats its subject virtually as a painter only . . .
>
> (R1 38,40)

It is not difficult to demonstrate that this is factually wrong. Gregory is introduced in the sixth stanza as 'Our Sidney and our perfect man', that is, as a Renaissance man, *uomo universale*, a man who excelled in both the active and contemplative arts; and the following four stanzas bear this out.

In the seventh stanza we meet a man extremely responsive to the beauties of nature and, the suggestion is, deeply attached to his home land. In the eighth stanza we meet the reckless (not foolhardy) horseman, and in the ninth a painter: in the tenth, a man whose omni-competence was such that he could have supervised all the practical artistry which is involved in composing the 'lovely intricacies of a house'. In short, of the forty-odd lines describing the accomplishments of Major Robert Gregory, 'Our Sidney and our perfect man', only five are concerned with the painter, and the line that is repeated three times is 'Soldier, scholar, horseman, he'.

Needless to say, Kermode's notion of Gregory is crucially important to his reading, for it enables him to see the line 'What made us dream that he could comb grey hair?' as consistent with the rest of the poem, instead of, as I maintain, significantly out of step. It is as if his reading of the eleventh stanza prevents him from seeing its incompatibility with the preceding four. However, since I disagree with Kermode at this fundamental level, I see nothing to be gained in pursuing him further.

APOCALYPTIC POEMS

> There is nothing behind the curtain other than that which
> is in front of it.
>
> (Hegel, transcribed by F. H. Bradley)

While Yeats was writing the Symbolist poems we considered
in the last chapter, Europe was consuming itself on a scale and
in a fashion which decisively eliminated any possibility of the
exiled courtier's return. What the war did offer Yeats, however,
was encouragement for the view — which he had in any case
been entertaining — that western civilization was finally
breaking up; and if he could align himself with *that* drama,
there might indeed be poems to write.

The essential prerequisite of good apocalyptic verse is a
theology or myth in terms of which one can perceive the
disaster as both necessary and just; that is to say, not ultimately
a disaster at all. Indeed for those whose vision is mythically
shaped, the denouement may be one of the least disturbing
parts of the story, like the duelling finale in *Hamlet*. In any
case, possession of the whole can protect one against
immoderate pain in the parts: it can also, however, exclude
one from the drama altogether. Yeats provides a nice example
of both possibilities in his breathtaking suggestion that 'We
should not attribute a very high degree of reality to the Great
War' (MM 282).

The reality which Yeats finds lacking in the Great War is
the larger perspective, the myth whose conclusion the war
merely illustrates. One might call such a myth 'a philosophy
of history', and though Yeats may have found his in
Nietzsche, its basic outline was a commonplace of Romantic
thought. Yeats's summary is admirable: 'Is not all history but
the coming of that conscious art which first makes articulate
and then destroys the old wild energy? ' (E1 372). In crude
Freudian terms, this is to say that cultures arise when ego and
super-ego conspire to create forms which regulate the chaotic
energies of the id. After a time, regulation becomes suppress-
ion, and energy atrophies: 'When a civilization ends, task
having led to task until everybody was bored, the whole
turns bottom upwards, Nietzsche's "transvaluation of all

58

values" ' (E 433). When the id can no longer tolerate the boredom it breaks up the forms, 'the old wild energy' returns, and the story begins again.

Much of Yeats's poetry is elegiac, in memory of past civility. But he was also a twentieth-century man, capable of being bored by all that. As such he could countenance the smash-up with some relief, even gaiety: for when the old gods go, we are set free, and this freedom can be as exhilarating as it is frightening. Regardless of whether Yeats really believed a new cycle of civilization would follow the cataclysms of the twentieth century, he found in them an abundance of material to engage his daemonic energies.

'Nineteen Hundred and Nineteen'

> And I would have all know that when all falls
> In ruin, poetry calls out in joy,
> Being the scattering hand, the bursting pod,
> The victim's joy among the holy flame,
> God's laughter at the shattering of the world.
>
> (CPL 114)

What is striking about this passage is that Yeats has poetry not just celebrating the world's dissolution but itself administering the alchemical kiss of death. The alchemist's ambition in this case is to overpower the seeming 'otherness' of historical developments, raise them to destiny as it were, and himself become the god-like author of his civilization's decline and fall. Not unlike Hegel's notion of the idealist philosopher who arises like Minerva's owl at dusk, he is both powerless to affect the course of history, and yet is the only one really in a position to *grasp* it, to be 'in at the death of the hare' (CP 251). Although Yeats frequently plays with such alchemical energies, nowhere does he do so with more vigour and conviction than in '1919'.

The poem opens with a fond invocation of the statues which civilized Athens. The 'ancient image' is the archaic aniconic woodcarving of *Athena Polias* in the Erectheum, which was worshipped annually in the Panathenian festival. Succeeding and in a sense competing with her was one of Phidias's most famous ivories, the chryselephantine *Athena Parthenos*, of whom Gombrich writes:

There was no doubt something almost primitive and
savage in some of its features . . . But already these
primitive ideas about the gods as formidable demons who
dwelt in the statues had ceased to be the main thing . . .
The Athena of Pheidias was like a great human being. Her
power lay less in any magic spells than in her beauty.
People realized at the time that the art of Pheidias had given
the people of Greece a new conception of the divine.[1]

The ornamental golden grasshoppers symbolized Athenian
decadence for Thucydides,[2] and recall the golden bird in
'Sailing to Byzantium' which takes

> . . . such a form as Grecian goldsmiths make
> Of hammered gold and gold enamelling
> To keep a drowsy Emperor awake.

(CP 218)

Gilded insects and birds are instances of organic forms which
have been perfected and travestied in the alchemical imagina-
tion, and their appearance at the end of the stanza completes
a progression of images (from olive wood through chrysele-
phantine warrior to golden grasshoppers) which captures
nicely Yeats's sense of 'all history' as 'the coming of that
conscious art which first makes articulate and then destroys
the old wild energy' (EI 372).[3] As the artistry grows less
savage and more ingenious, energy dissipates and *polis* life
erodes, for 'If human violence is not embodied in our
institutions the young will not give them their affection, nor
the young and old their loyalty' (E 441). The punning
reference to 'common things' reminds us that sacred things
(such as the statues) which create and inform the common
places, in the end become commonplace: and when the old
wild energy returns, some incendiary can be found 'to burn
that stump on the Acropolis'.
   The second and third stanzas suggest that late nineteenth-
century England was kept awake by pretty toys comparable
to the Athenians' grasshoppers and bees. Just as the magic of
Athena's statues achieved the political stability which made

1. E. H. Gombrich, *The Story of Art*, p. 57.

2 See *History of the Peloponnesian War*, Book One, Chapter 1, para. 6.

3. Cf. 'Every movement, in feeling or in thought, prepares in the dark by its own
   increasing clarity and confidence its own executioner' (M 340).

possible the ingenious lovely things 'that seemed sheer miracle to the multitude' ('more miracle than bird of handiwork' as Yeats describes the changeless metal in 'Byzantium') so the pomp and circumstance of empire convinced England that Pax Britannica would 'outlive all future days'; and this drowsy conviction made possible the 'fine thought' of the *fin de siécle* aesthetes. Those who noticed that the cannons were still loaded and occasionally fired must have thought it was simply a measure to preserve the spunkiness of the circus animals. They had probably forgotten that the histrionics of potency will not always suffice, and that man's sacred rage, his lust and his fear, periodically require the burning of more than a little powder.

This requirement is fulfilled in the fourth stanza when the drowsy chargers give way to the night mare; clearly the 'old wild energy' has returned:

> The night can sweat with terror as before
> We pieced our thoughts into philosophy,
> And planned to bring the world under a rule,
> Who are but weasels fighting in a hole.

This passage is echoed and its meanings amplified in 'Meru', a sonnet written some fourteen years later:

> Civilization is hooped together, brought
> Under a rule, under the semblance of peace
> By manifold illusion; but man's life is thought,
> And he, despite his terror, cannot cease
> Ravening through century after century,
> Ravening, raging, and uprooting that he may come
> Into the desolation of reality.

These lines in turn are admirably glossed in a passage from *Autobiographies*: 'All civilization is held together by the suggestions of an invisible hypnotist — by artificially created illusions. The knowledge of reality is always in some measure a secret knowledge. It is a kind of death' (A 482). Artist-magicians make suggestions such as the statues of Athena whereby a semblance of peace is achieved. But man's thought (not just his action) is twofold in its tendency, and periodically requires the return of the primordial terror. The

Hermits on Mount Meru, in mockery of those who pieced their thoughts into philosophy, sit 'caverned in night under the drifted snow'. They strikingly resemble Wallace Stevens's 'Snow Man' who has 'been cold a long time' and is

> . . . the listener, who listens in the snow,
> And, nothing himself, beholds
> Nothing that is not there and the nothing that is.

When a culture is flourishing, the artist-magicians are the invisible hypnotists who create the illusions of stability and beauty. When the time comes for these illusions to be shattered, they repair to the holy mountains for meditation upon the desolation of reality.

The fifth stanza of '1919' ends rather obscurely, but Yeats seems to be hoping that if he can move his mind to such a mountain he might be spared the pain of being violently dispossessed. If he can disposses *himself* of the comforts of civilization he would have

> but one comfort left: all triumph would
> But break upon his ghostly solitude.

It is an intelligible aspiration, and we have already seen in the last chapter that as a ghostly poet he was excluded from various kinds of human suffering.

But in this poem he is by no means convinced that such detachment is possible, for in the very next line he asks

> But is there any comfort to be found?
> Man is in love and loves what vanishes,
> What more is there to say?

This is to say not only that mutability is the case, but that man's love is not exhausted until it has destroyed the very miracles it has worshipped. Our fascination with the golden light that falls from the grasshoppers and bees finds its consummation only in the flames that consume them. This is the dance we all must dance, and any talk of sitting it out in ghostly solitude is just talk; for even the most apparently indifferent spectator will be taking some secret delight in the devastation. This thought does not completely surface until section IV; but it is obliquely registered in these stanzas, and Yeats brings it nearer in section II when he concludes that

> *All* men are dancers and their tread
> Goes to the barbarous clangour of a gong.

He returns to the question of ghostly solitude in the rather low-keyed section III where he compares the soul to a swan. Situated *in* the worldly element of water but not *of* it, the swan may choose to play upon its surface: alternatively, as its arched wings indicate, it can leap into the heavens when the water's surface grows either tedious or turbulent. Equally at home in both elements, it is tied to neither. Yeats finds this an attractive image for the solitary soul; but he also finds it 'troubled' by the body, which tends to get attached to things. This is true not only of our physical bodies, but also of the metaphysical bodies we build in art and politics. Because we stick to our bodies, we are always in danger of getting stuck. This is particularly true in times of civil war, when our bodies both physical and metaphysical are exposed to violence.

The weather has now grown foul, and 'The swan has leaped into the desolate heaven'. We may try to emulate him, by writing Symbolist poetry, for instance, which refines the body into pure spirit. But such poetry is only magic, a kind of illusion, since even its finest ecstasies are temporary: however sublime the evening was, we must get up for breakfast in the morning. Our inability to match the swan's flight in poetry is aptly registered in 'The half-imagined, the half-written page'; and this failure can bring panic and a rage to destroy all those things in and through which we are grounded — in effect, 'all things', even the half-written page through which we had hoped to escape: that is to say, this poem. At this point Yeats's 'wildness' has very nearly rendered him speechless; for the five lines with which he limps to the end of the section only recapitulate points already made, and simply ignore the wildness which the swan has unleashed.

The next section, only four lines long, seems to emerge slowly in the first two lines from deep depression — no adjectives, no colour, no metaphor:

> We, who seven years ago
> Talked of honour and of truth,

Shriek with pleasure if we show
The weasel's twist, the weasel's tooth.

Once again Yeats is thinking about the lofty pretensions of
artists and intellectuals; and he savages them in the second
two lines. Coming immediately after the failure to leap with
the swan, this passage recognizes the price we must pay for
such *hubris*. The failure to rise above it all leaves one degraded
indeed; as Yeats says earlier, we are 'but weasels fighting in a
hole'. More simply put, in times of civil war everyone's blood
is aroused; and though the mental people may have less blood
to arouse than soldiers do, this means only that their vicious-
ness comes out twisted.[4]

While the weasels shriek, the soldiers are trafficking in
physical destruction on a grand scale. Perhaps because Yeats
is heavily committed to a cyclical view of history (embarrass-
ingly symbolized in section II by Loie Fuller's Chinese
dancers)[5] which insists on the inevitability of their coming,
he seems able to countenance their activities with remarkable
equanimity.[6] But in any case, they are in the foreground,
and his principal concern is focused further back, on the
complicity of the weasels off stage. As a sometime thinker of
fine thoughts, a mocker 'who would not lift a hand' and who
shrieks with pleasure at the devastation, he traffics in
nihilistic sacrilege as much as the drunken soldiery and those
who sacked the Acropolis. Thus in an age of apocalyptic

---

4. The image of the weasel for the artist-magicians who supervise both the
   illusions which create cultural stability and the knowledge which dismantles
   them becomes more convincing in view of Lady Gregory's report that 'they
   are enchanted and understand all things' (C 276).

5. Embarrassing, I think, because an unsuccessful attempt on the widespread
   practice of seeing the world not in a grain of sand but in the forms of
   commerce — the origin of Pop Art. One thinks for example of Satie's furniture
   music and Mallarme's interest in the cubism of the newspaper. Closer to home
   was Arthur Symons's metaphysical interest in the music hall. In this sense at
   least Yeats lacked the common touch. One is almost fond of the grumly gyres
   because they seem appropriate to a lonely Irish mind constructed of shreds
   and patches; but Loie Fuller's dragon of air, particularly in this astringent
   poem, is an alien presence.

6. In fact, he barely mentions them. The closest he comes to objecting is in the
   fourth stanza of section I. However, I hear quiet exultation rather than out-
   rage in these lines, which release their tension on 'scot-free' — the cold
   nonchalance of the horseman turned nasty perhaps. Yeats admits such
   brutalization in the two poems which precede '1919' (CP 230-2).

polarization, an oblique kind of passionate intensity infects even those who lack all conviction.[7] Yeats is suggesting that the sound of shrieking *clercs* is distressingly similar to the roaring of the soldiers, which may even be preferable because more explicit. Although there is no direct comparison of the weasels with the drunken soldiery in this poem, the fifth and seventh sections of the preceding one find him locked in the tower, 'caught in the cold snows of a dream', and almost envious of the soldiers' play in the sun.

Section V completes the history of the mind's declension from miracle to mockery. This history ends in the attempt to 'mock mockers after that'. At this point of total degradation, when even one's mockery is up for sale, the human spirit seems on the verge of self-cancellation. And yet, though it may be the moment of death, it may also be the moment of transfiguration. For if human history is about to expire in the final section's dance of death, then the rage to end all things is no mere hopeless fantasy but an imminent possibility; and if the solitary soul can identify with that rage, it may join the swan after all, and 'ride the winds that clamour of approaching night'. This is indeed a wild idea, and the only way to tell if it is on Yeats's mind is to consider carefully the poem's concluding section.

*

As a presentation of the contemporary apocalyptic sensibility, this concluding piece is both accurate and inspired. For those of us brought up on 'bomb culture', the 'sudden blast of dusty wind' has an unmistakably nuclear tang, and it refers to an explosion that has already occurred in many minds. When the dust settles, of course, it is all over. Nevertheless, there are some not utterly absorbed in the complacency of the 'indifferent multitude' envisaged in the previous poem, and they make one last effort to compose some vision out of the 'mere images' that litter the almost deserted stage. But the best they can manage is a revival of black magic, the worship of a phantom since reality has left them. We have come a long way from the ingenious lovely things that seemed to civilize the multitude with miracle in the opening lines; indeed we have come full circle.[8]

7. As Nietzsche puts it, 'Man would sooner have the void for his purpose than be void of purpose' (*Genealogy of Morals*, III, section 28).

What is remarkable and troubling about Yeats's conclusion is that it leaves us feeling exhilarated, not frightened or depressed. This can be partially explained by the two figures who appear at the end. Artisson and Kyteler are old and Irish and extravagant; which makes them friends to Yeats, and hence to us. It seems that this energetic lady from Kilkenny managed to dispatch four of her husbands in the fourteenth century before she was indicted for consorting with her singularly cretinous and lower-class incubus. As a handsome Anglo-Norman aristocrat her presence here reminds us that Yeats's paradigm of Western decadence involves upper-class ladies coupling with lower-class men; and as patron saint of Irish witches her presence here suggests that twentieth-century witchcraft need not be altogether unimaginative. In sum, she brightens a decidedly dark scene with her 'bronzed peacock feathers' and makes it less disturbing by giving it both pedigree and historical precedent. Indeed she may be gesturing towards a new cycle; for if Artisson is the slouching beast, then she may represent the twentieth-century Leda, about to conceive something outrageous for the next millenium. But even though these two figures are marvellously poetical, they do not altogether enhance the poem; for they distract us from the banality of evil in our time, surely its peculiar horror. Had Yeats reserved some of his mockery for those who fancied *badness* might be gay, he might have had second thoughts about giving us the devil in fancy dress.

The second principal source of the strange exhilaration in the finale is more difficult to judge. To put it crudely, is this poetry *about* hysteria or is the writing itself hysterical? As a set piece of gothic fantasy it certainly differs markedly from the preceding sections; for all its violence no one is in pain, and the 'crazy hand' which may be interfering with daughters strikes us more as an intriguing possibility than as something horrible. By contrast, the figure in section V

> That would not lift a hand maybe
> To help good, wise or great
> To bar that foul storm out

takes on considerable gravity from its simple and monosyllabic presentation; for all its inactivity the mocking hand has substance, whereas the 'crazy hand' only shimmers.

---

8. As we do in the preceding poem, whose apocalyptic finale also includes the *revanche* of a fourteenth-century witch.

Thus the objection to section VI must be that it abandons five sections of sustained high seriousness for apocalyptic fantasy which may be to some extent pornographic. However, it may also be that Yeats can answer this charge simply by agreeing wholeheartedly. Section V, he might argue, effectively concludes the poem: the history of morality terminates in the impasse from which we traffic in mockery. What comes after that is a postscript, a manic condition in which *all* are blind. When all men are fantasists, the distinction between inner and outer, between 'thunder of feet' and 'tumult of images', breaks down: no longer capable of acting upon an objective realm (which has in any case disappeared) man becomes subject only to the images that flash upon his screen — to which he responds with amorous cries or angry cries, as the moment moves him.

In sum, section VI *presents* us with a brief experience of apocalyptic mania. And if one grants that the mimesis is well done, as one surely must, there can be no question of the writing being itself hysterical. Hence one's objection to it must be either that this is not the way the world ends, or that if it is, our exposure to it can only bring the date nearer. Since 1919 all the arts have become almost obsessively apocalyptic, and the arguments for and against such experience these days tend to be rather like the arguments for and against taking drugs. Those in favour tend to claim that apocalyptic madness is in the air and small doses can be innoculative; or more simply, that since apocalypse is nigh one should bear witness and damn the torpedoes. Those against tend to argue that both the passionately intense and those who lack conviction are whoring after apocalypse, which has nothing to do with the ineluctable logic of world-history and everything to do with malice and self-indulgence. Needless to say there is substance in both arguments, and fanatics on either side are unconvincing. In the case of '1919' I am marginally *for*, though it is unfortunately the sort of decision each reader must make for himself.

Finally we must look at the conclusion in the light of the leaping swan and Yeats's rage to end all things. Any suggestion that Yeats has finally subdued his rage and agreed humbly to finish the dance must, I think, be resisted; for there is no indication that the final frenzy touches him at all. Indeed quite the reverse: it is the one section from which the poet as protagonist is strikingly absent. It is also the section in which the verse is manifestly thriving on destruction. Relevant here is the passage discussed at the outset (p. 58):

> And I would have all know that when all falls
> In ruin, poetry calls out in joy,
> Being the scattering hand, the bursting pod . . .

One must, I think, conclude that section VI is calling out in joy because the rage to end all things has finally found its form, and by means of these energies Yeats hopes at last to 'cast off body and trade' and join the desolated swan.

As an Irishman, a weasel, and a trafficker in mockery, Yeats has gone under with the rest. But as the exuberance in the writing would suggest, he does not fear this *Untergang*, for he is also the Symbolist mage authorizing the catastrophe. As such he can register a total condition from which there is no exit, and thereby escapes it. Thus the ultimate source of exhilaration lies in the poet's belief that as he ends this poem, no longer 'half-written', his words have become indistinguishable from 'God's laughter at the shattering of the world.'

It must be one of the word-magician's most dazzling performances; but as is so often the case with Yeats, we can only submit to his spell if we disagree with his Platonist about the body's stickiness, and believe that its ancient habit can be cast off when the words are right.

'Lapis Lazuli' (1936)

Although this poem was written many years after '1919', once again we find Yeats provoked by warfare into an attempt at defining his ironic posture. The crucial difference is in the elegant orientalism of 'Lapis Lazuli', through which Yeats would be spared the painful implications of time present, so vigorously confronted in '1919'. The attempt is not entirely successful, for the argument is muddled and at the end the beautiful Chinamen remain somewhat elusive. But this search for passage to the east is no vulgar piece of *chinoiserie*, and takes us through some of Yeats's finest writing.

A superficial reading suggests that 'Lapis Lazuli' is a characteristically Yeatsian meditation on twentieth-century apocalypse, perhaps more frivolous than usual, but charming certainly. Western civilization is about to be consumed in the violence of its self-destructive energies, the ancient tragic rhythm is being enacted once again, and even though the golden grasshoppers and bees are doomed, the only sane thing to do is enjoy while they last such old 'ingenious lovely things' as the lapis lazuli and the poem which praises it. Closer scrutiny, however, reveals both unsuspected complexity and, unfortunately, some confusion — though perhaps faulty perspective is unavoidable in a short poem which attempts to situate Hamlet, Lear, the Second World War and two ancient orientals on a common ground.

The first stanza is intriguing because it is not immediately apparent who is describing the coming war in such jolly terms. In early drafts a fairly sober description of the women's apprehensions is followed by the announcement that we, the gay poets, mindful of the heroic example of Hamlet and Lear, shall not 'break up our lines to weep'. In the final version this dramatic exchange is masterfully condensed in an ironic passage which I take to be the gay poet aping the frivolity of which the women accuse him, indicating — through his hyperbolic language — that there is more to his gaiety than meets the eye of these hysterical creatures, solemn sentimentalists presumably, with no conception of the profound philosophical understanding, suffering even, which underlies it. The implication then is that the poet's gaiety (described in terms appropriate to the coarseness of the present age) is a reasonable twentieth-century equivalent to Hamlet's 'the readiness is all'.

One resists this implication because the irony informing the send-up of the hysterical women is the only evidence we have of the poet's attitudes, and if he is to be Hamlet's peer we need some indication that his irony is the response to a comparable despair: name-dropping is not enough. In other words one cannot have the serenity of Act V without the anguish which precedes it; and if by the end of the poem the reader is still unsatisfied, as I am, that Acts I to IV have been implicitly accounted for, then he may conclude that the hysterical women's rebuke has not been satisfactorily discounted.

The theatrical irony which Yeats is commending in this poem as a response to the world theatre is briefly this: man is a *play-ful* animal and his war games are no exception to this rule. Although human play has a self-destructive 'tragic' tendency, *homo ludens* can survive his games and the sorrow they produce by holding fast to his perception of their playful character; or rather, since they may require the forfeit of his corporeal existence, he may transcend in the spirit what appears to be messy defeat in the body: hence the redemptive power of 'gaiety transfiguring all that dread'. [9] There is nothing intrinsically offensive or foolish about these ideas (which again have a very Nietzschean flavour), indeed they have a more general currency today than they did in the thirties. One's objections are rather to the way Yeats uses them in this poem.

The problems begin with his curious treatment of tragedy. In what may seem an uncharacteristically egalitarian gesture he proposes that Hamlet and Lear are everyman. In a less manic mood he would be the first to point out that much of the tragic quality of Hamlet and Lear lies in their being possessed to an unnatural degree of certain passions which arise less forcefully in mortal men; and that the purity of their heroic isolation is in contrast to the obscure complexity of the societies which isolate them; and that tragic art is art because it concentrates nature. But on this occasion such considerations are not to the point, which is basically to undermine the distinctions between art and life by seeing that everyone's life is a play, a tragic play in fact, indeed the *same* tragic play. By means of this nihilistic perception which reduces all history to one-dimensional monochrome, Yeats concentrates our attention upon the vanity of human wishes, and thus implicitly commends those virtues which may arise from broken dreams: stoicism, composure, lucidity, a profoundly superficial gaiety.

Although the meanings in the second and third sections are difficult to trace, they seem to be giving an account of western tragedy as seen by the Chinamen. All lives and indeed all civilizations perform a tragic play; viewed with sufficiently elevated detachment, all these plays reveal a similar form: 'All men have aimed at, found, and lost.' In the end, there is one story and one story only, and the acceptance of its eternal recurrence is the height of wisdom. Although Hamlet, Lear, Ophelia and Cordelia may seem to be working through

9. The actor of course transcends *in corpore* as well. When the curtain falls, he arises, thereby providing a humorous allegorical demonstration of how a man can survive his roles by not investing all his substance in them.

quite different sorts of experience, the Chinamen know better; and even if the curtains were to fall simultaneously 'upon a hundred thousand stages', as indeed they did at Hiroshima, the story remains the same, for 'It cannot grow by an inch or an ounce'. Thus from the top of the metaphysical mountain, the answer to the hysterical women down below is, if not 'Rejoice!', at least 'Relax — history is not — cannot be — about to play new tricks; for we have known it all already'.

Once one sees that the poem's intention is to compare the gaiety of occidental tragedy with that of oriental wisdom, to the detriment of the former, the puzzling tone of the second stanza becomes less puzzling. In suggesting that Hamlet 'struts' and 'rambles' and 'all the drop-scenes drop', Yeats is calling attention to the grotesque, violent, even insane aspects of tragic passion, which contrast sharply with the elegant composure of the Chinamen. Occidental tragedy can produce a kind of gaiety, but the emphasis is on the hero's struggle to preserve the illusion of his individuality and make it prevail, an emphasis which the staring orientals must find regrettable. Thus Hamlet and Lear are marvellous in their way, but they do rage somewhat incontinently for a prominent part in the play, and take a long time to realize that since the play's a sad and repetitive thing, the *best* thing is to get off the stage as soon as possible: ' . . . no Hamlets, full of their own selves, passionate for knowledge, but only monks with empty eyeballs, contemplating, like the Buddhists, nothingness.' [10] In view of the banal sameness of all historical struggle, Yeats would perhaps like to resign his part in the casual tragedy, escape his occidental destiny as a minor Hamlet or Lear, and exchange their gaiety, a transcendence of sorts, for the more durable, less hysterical variety enjoyed by the orientals. [11] In an earlier poem he put it this way:

Never to have lived is best, ancient writers say; . . .
The second best's a gay goodnight and quickly turn away.

(CP 255)

10. Cited in C 494.

11. Lear clings to Cordelia to the end, and the question of his gaiety is even more problematic than Hamlet's. Such gaiety as he musters lies in 'Come, let's away to prison'. However, the fact that Yeats is here giving an utterly inadequate account of western tragedy is so obvious that it needs no arguing.

Such an abstract view of history and the spirit of western tragedy as we find in the second section is unconvincing to say the least, and the poet's loss of control is manifest, for example in the lifeless frenzy of

Black out; Heaven blazing into the head:
Tragedy wrought to its uttermost.

The unease and rant which run throughout this section contrast markedly with the extraordinary distinction of the latter part of the poem, in which the simple delicacy of the Chinamen is rendered with conviction and subtlety. Indeed, one feels that the Chinamen would want no part of the generalized waffle which precedes their appearance, that although they would certainly be perplexed by the excesses of Hamlet and Lear, they would not put it so; for it is the outstanding virtue of a disciplined nihilism such as theirs that, paradoxically, it can release one from the noisy aggressiveness of abstract speculation and send one back to the world of details — 'accomplished fingers' after all, measure time with care. Having stared upon Alpha and Omega, having traced the distant outline of mountain and sky, the old men may return to a foreground from which 'accomplished fingers begin to play'. It is a profoundly arresting composition, and particularly attractive to us today, living as we must in the shadow of the megabomb.

It is important to emphasize the difference between the Chinamen and the hermits we find on Mount Meru a few pages earlier. They may all be on the same mountain, but the Chinamen are moving towards the half-way house, whereas the hermits are 'caverned' in the snows on the top. Although the Chinamen are certainly aware of the snow, their nihilism is sweetened by 'plum or cherry branch' and the melodies that register their passing.[12] The half-way house is their palace of art, an inclusive irony that mediates between the mutable foreground and the nothingness of God. Because they keep one eye 'on the mountain and the sky', they are not tempted to overestimate the significance of man's ambition; and so their palace is 'a little half-way house', with none of the gaudy rhetoric of Tennyson's baroque folly. Although they are some distance from 'the tragic scene', they are labouring

12.   Cf. EI 431 where Yeats points out that eastern mystics differ from western in the delight they often take in the sensible world.

up the mountain, and time will continue to wrinkle their bodies until they reach the lofty snows. In view of such *ascesis*, there is nothing unseemly or voyeuristic in their asking for mournful melodies; and their ancient gaiety, to my mind at any rate, reveals an attractive alternative to the *gigantesque* of occidental tragedy.

Some sense of what 'Lapis Lazuli' leaves out in its fascination with the Chinamen's composure can be gathered from Eliot's 'Burnt Norton', which is also concerned with nihilism as a discipline through which historical suffering may be redeemed. What distinguishes Eliot's poem is its vivid awareness of the ties that bind us to the contingencies of history. Whereas 'Lapis Lazuli' says nothing of the difficulties of disengaging from the historical stage (nor indeed of climbing the mountain) 'Burnt Norton' speaks of little else:

> Yet the enchainment of past and future
> Woven in the weakness of the changing body,
> Protects mankind from heaven and damnation
> Which flesh cannot endure.

Only in the context of such enchainment, experienced *as such* and not as a philosophical abstraction, can one appreciate the difficulties envisaged by such a line as 'Only through time time is conquered', and the nature of the desire for such conquest.

The view that in this poem Yeats was trying to correct the misplaced emphasis of western tragedy in the light of oriental quietism, or better, find some synthesis of the two, gains some support from a letter he wrote in 1935 describing the piece of lapis lazuli on which the poem is based:

> . . . someone has sent me a present of a great piece carved by some Chinese sculptor into the semblance of a mountain with temple, trees, paths, and an ascetic and pupil about to climb the mountain. Ascetic, pupil, hard stone, eternal theme of the sensual east. The heroic cry in the midst of despair. But no, I am wrong, the east has its solutions always and therefore knows nothing of tragedy. It is we, not the east, that must raise the heroic cry.
> (LDW 8)

Yeats's first impulse is to see the Chinamen as similar to occidental figures for whom some participation in life's tragedy is inescapable. Implicated in the suffering they contemplate, their serenity can be interpreted, like Hamlet's and Lear's, as the heroic cry in the midst of despair. But then he remembers that oriental mysticism is based upon the disengagement from history and all her works, and that for them such disengagement is pursued as a daily discipline, not just a momentary black-out of the joys and sorrows engaged on the historical stage. In a tone that recalls his half-reluctant rejection of Von Hügel (CP 286), Yeats turns away from the east and returns to his business with the heroic cry. It is possible that in writing the poem a year later, his admiration for the dignity of oriental nihilism made him forget his distinction between oriental and occidental sensibilities, and construe the Chinamen's gaiety simply as a more sublime form of Hamlet's and Lear's heroism. By conflating the two sensibilities in this way, the ageing poet could cling to the heroic tradition while being spared its frenzy — in which case one can see 'An Acre of Grass', written three months later, as to some extent an act of contrition for the 'quietness' of 'Lapis Lazuli'.

However, there is in the last section one admirably subtle indication that Yeats is aware of the distance that separates east from west:

Every discoloration of the stone,
Every accidental crack or dent,
Seems a water-course or an avalanche,
Or lofty slope where it still snows . . .

Such accidents can be interpreted as irrelevant to the timeless scene depicted, details which only a time-haunted westerner like the poet might think part of the picture. To him they even suggest the potential violence of an avalanche. The Chinamen, however, know that such 'accidents' are not part of their reality. But since the poet notices these details and tends to find them significant, even threatening, we may suppose that his delight in their gaiety is somewhat uneasy, that he cannot make it completely his own. In the end then, he has joined the Chinamen, but still speaks with a noticeably western accent.

This poem, though largely written from the Chinamen's point of view, is, necessarily, the work of a twentieth-century word-magician. This can be discerned in the description of Callimachus's handiwork:

No handiwork of Callimachus,
Who handled marble as if it were bronze,
Made draperies that seemed to rise
When sea-wind swept the corner, stands.

The magic in the sculptor's hand whereby he modelled stone that seemed timelessly to move in time is not unlike the magic in the poet's hand whereby the antinomies of day and night may be summoned and composed in a time and space which are neither.

The crucial difference of course is that language, being more immaterial than stone (either more or less substantial depending on one's metaphysic) is that much more intrinsically magical. Whereas the sculptor 'creates or reveals' life in stone, the poet arguably both creates his life and as the poem ends, destroys it. Callimachus launches his stone children into the world and their execution is determined by another. The poem on the contrary, in so far as it never actually penetrates the world of space and time, is both still-born and indestructible. By summoning life out of nothing and returning it there, the poet imitates God; on the other hand, he must be fairly constantly perplexed in his attempts to construe *Nihil ex nihilo fit*.

In his treatment of Callimachus one senses Yeats quietly brandishing this ultimate power to play with the paradoxes of life and death. 'No handiwork of Callimachus', which he then lovingly resurrects, 'stands'; and in that solid substantiating word, the sculpture's disappearance is ordered and registered. It is a marvellous passage, perhaps as characteristic of the poet-magus as anything Yeats wrote. In any case, it clearly reveals the crucible of irony and nihilism from which this extremely elegant poem springs.

THE SPIDER'S EYE

In the spiritual dawn when Raphael painted the Camera della Segnatura . . . Europe might have . . . begun the solution of its problems, but individualism came instead; the egg instead of hatching, burst.

(EI 467)

Already in mid-Renaissance the world was weary of wisdom, science began to appear in the elaborate perspectives of its painters, in their sense of weight and tangibility; man was looking for some block where he could lay his head.

(E 436)

For though love has a spider's eye
To find out some appropriate pain —
Aye, though all passion's in the glance —

(CP 199)

In the opening years of the twentieth century Yeats had studied Renaissance courtesy with great pleasure, and envied the happy poets who, as he thought, had lived in such civilized times that they could participate actively in their society's life as courtiers, and celebrate that life openly in arts which were 'but the point of the spear whose handle is our daily life' (E 212).[1]

The poems examined thus far, however, have shown us a solitary poet more concerned with the dead than the living. Finding little to commend in the present, he elegizes the past; and when he does deal with the contemporary world he shows us its deadliness, its refusal to tolerate the good, the true and the beautiful. He is not simply a historian who records what's gone, but a Symbolist mage who finds in the recording process a liveliness which life lacks, and which to uninitiated eyes looks deathly, if not perverse and ghoulish.

The difference between these two kinds of poetry is very considerable — like the difference between realism and idealism — and since Yeats would have preferred to write the first kind, it is not surprising that he took pains to understand the historical conditions which had forced would-be

---

1. This phrase is from a passage which appears as epigraph to this book.

courtier poets like himself to become Symbolist specialists in death. But more than curiosity was involved: he knew that his 'deathly' practice had its roots in an inherited sense of cultural defeat, and that if he were not to make matters worse he must study that defeat and the various ways in which modern man has attempted to survive it. It is a study that we too should find worth undertaking, not only to gain critical perspective on the kind of poetry Yeats wrote, but more generally to understand better the difficulties that obstruct our own survival.

Symbolism is of course a product of late Romanticism, but the story begins much further back when the modern arts began to grow old and unhappy. Since Yeats believed the Renaissance courtier was the last of the happy poets, one would expect him to look for the origins of modern unhappiness in the late Renaissance when the age of courtesy passed away; and so he does. It was during that fateful time, with the courts dispersing and the Christian god in decline, that the social fabric was irreparably torn and the arts began to 'perfect themselves away from life' (E 212). Like many before him and since, Yeats believed this was a profoundly significant development, and that modern unhappiness was conceived around 1600 when individualism was born.

At the basis of individualism is a new definition of the relations between man and his surroundings. If a man stands alone he tends to stand hostile, expecting the world to put him down if he does not dominate it. One way he can seek such domination is through knowledge: if he can, through some form of contemplative word-magic, create a mental reproduction of the world, it will cease to be alien and other, and become his possession, part of himself. If he does this, however, he may be not just dominating the world, but killing it off in some sense; for we have already seen that in certain respects, the ideal is to the real as death is to life. Such activity may well prove to be related to the Symbolist poet's attempt to know the world through words which end it in a book.

In what follows I shall attempt to expound and amplify Yeats's notion of modern man's cognitive designs on the world. The figure that will emerge is that of a spider; and since he tries to take the world in by imagining it in images, a discussion of what goes on in the spider's eye is properly called an essay on perception.

*

Both in his poetry and prose, Yeats's protraits concentrate on the eyes. Their iconic importance arises from the crucial information they provide concerning their owner's interest in and dependence upon his surroundings; for example, one of the most significant distinctions in Yeats's thought is contained in the contrast between narrowed eyes, hungry for nourishment from the external world, and those which are open and staring, full of their own dream of either plenitude or vacancy. This is ultimately a mythic distinction — between Adam in the garden, intuitively connected to its inhabitants, and Adam fallen into history and self-estrangement, looking to others for confirmation and clarification of his diminished self. In short, when Adam loses touch with his body 'The garden dies' (CP 240), and his eyes, no longer outlets of the body's energy, take on a piercing look which is unmistakably intellectual.

It will come as no surprise that one of Yeats's most important illustrations of this difference involves an Italian courtier:

In the Dublin National Gallery there hung, perhaps there still hang, upon the same wall, a portrait of some Venetian gentleman by Strozzi, and Mr. Sargent's painting of President Wilson. Whatever thought broods in the dark eyes of that Venetian gentleman has drawn its life from his whole body; it feeds upon it as the flame feeds upon the candle — and should that thought be changed, his pose would change, his very cloak would rustle, for his whole body thinks. President Wilson lives only in the eyes, which are steady and intent; the flesh about the mouth is dead, and the hands are dead, and the clothes suggest no movement of his body, nor any movement but that of the valet, who has brushed and folded in mechanical routine.

(A 292)

Yeats also finds a fall in the movement from Greece to Rome, as he explains in a marvellous passage lamenting 'the scrupulous realism' which led the Roman sculptors to 'drill a round hole to represent the pupil':

When I think of Rome I see always those heads with their world-considering eyes, and those bodies as conventional as the metaphors in a leading article, and compare in my

imagination vague Grecian eyes gazing at nothing, Byzantine
eyes of drilled ivory staring upon a vision, and those eye-
lids of China and of India, those veiled or half-veiled eyes
weary of world and vision alike.

(AV 277)

Just as the Romans finished off the Greeks, so the aggressive
acquisitiveness of the late Renaissance, whose spiritual spokes-
man is Hamlet, put an end to the self-delighting reverie of
the preceding era. Referring to a portrait of William Morris
by Watts, Yeats writes:

Its grave wide-open eyes, like the eyes of some dreaming
beast, remind me of the open eyes of Titian's *Ariosto,*
while the broad vigorous body suggests a mind that has
no need of the intellect to remain sane, though it give itself
to every fantasy: the dreamer of the Middle Ages. It is 'the
fool of Faery . . . wide and wild as a hill', the resolute
European image that yet half remembers Buddha's motion-
less meditation, and has no trait in common with the
wavering, lean image of hungry speculation, that cannot
but because certain famous Hamlets of our stage fill
the mind's eye. Shakespeare himself foreshadowed a sym-
bolic change, that is, a change in the whole temperament
of the world, for though he called his Hamlet 'fat' and
even 'scant of breath', he thrust between his fingers agile
rapier and dagger.

(A 141-2)

In this passage, hungry speculation is Hamlet's defining feature
(elsewhere Yeats describes him as 'passionate for knowledge'
[C 494]) and this hunger is associated with, even symbolized
by, the agile rapier and dagger which are thrust between his
fingers. In 'The Statues' we learn more of this hunger when
we meet a 'Hamlet thin from eating flies'. When we combine
this image with the long lethal fingers in the above passage,
Yeats's Hamlet begins to look like a spider.

Yeats uses this very image in a chilling description of the
modern poet:

Fly-catchers of the moon,
Our hands are blenched, our fingers seem

But slender needles of bone;
Blenched by that malicious dream
They are spread wide that each
May rend what comes in reach.

(CP 273)

To my mind this is one of Yeats's finest stanzas; and in this
context it prompts us to discover what is spidery about the
hunger for speculation which afflicts both Hamlet and
modern poets, and how it differs from the empty eyeballs
enjoyed by the fat dreamer of the Middle Ages. This question
is a difficult one, and the attempt to answer it in the next
few pages will have to be somewhat abstract and cryptic if
we are to avoid being drawn into a full discussion of idealist
epistemology and the dissociation of sensibility. Such a
discussion would take us too far from Yeats, whose dealings
with such weighty matters, though usually very shrewd, are
always brisk and amateur.

*

In the late nineteenth century many thinkers were fascinated
by Hamlet, by the way his function was smothered in surmise
of a relentlessly metaphysical nature. Nietzsche put it this
way:

Dionysiac man might be said to resemble Hamlet: both
have looked deeply into the true nature of things, they
have *understood* and are now loath to act. They realise
that no action of theirs can work any change in the eternal
condition of things, and they regard the imputation as
ludicrous or debasing that they should set right the time
which is out of joint.

(BT 51)

For both Nietzsche and Yeats, Hamlet's chief significance is
his mistrust of appearances, his refusal to take part in a play
whose meanings he had not mastered. As Nietzsche put it,
his desire is to 'tear asunder the veil of Maya' (BT 27), to
penetrate the delusive surfaces and find the reality under-
neath. He is thin because he is haunted by the ideal — that
remembered or imagined perfection which prevents his being
at home in an unfinished world, and which 'can bring a rage

to end all things'. More simply, he refuses to feed his too too solid flesh with apples which might contain worms; as he says to the king, 'I eat the air promise-crammed, you cannot feed a capon so'.

Although the evil that worries Hamlet is moral as well as metaphysical, it is the latter kind which concerns us here, for it is his unnatural appetites which make him, in the eyes of both Nietzsche and Yeats, typically 'modern'. It is worth taking some trouble over this notion of Hamlet and the modern, because Yeats, as he occasionally admits, is also infected by it; indeed, most of my criticisms of his poetry concern the distortions of otherness resulting from his spidery rage for essence, a rage which he claims modern man has learned from Hamlet.

There is widespread agreement amongst those with a mythic interest in history that soon after 1600, Adam re-enacted the Fall: in Yeats's words, 'Imagination, whether in literature, painting, or sculpture, sank after the death of Shakespeare' (EI 396).[2] While there are many versions of this story — T. S. Eliot's for example is called 'The Dissociation of Sensibility' — the better ones recognize that philosophy must play a prominent part; indeed, some of them begin, as Yeats put it, with 'that morning when Descartes discovered that he could think better in his bed than out of it' (A 192). Boileau put it even more succinctly when he said that Descartes had cut poetry's throat.

Hannah Arendt agrees with Yeats that 'Modern philosophy began with Descartes's *de omnibus dubitandum est*... In modern philosophy and thought, doubt occupies much the same central position as that occupied for all the centuries before by the Greek *thaumazein,* the wonder at everything that is as it is' (HC 249). She goes on to connect this doubt with the rise of modern science:

2. It is worth emphasizing that in these pages I am more concerned with myth than history. Like most myths, this version of the Fall is both historical and a-historical; both about what happened (once upon a time) and what happens. Clearly the question of historical accuracy is an important one, but for present purposes, not pre-eminently so. Thus in what follows, my first concern is expository; only infrequently shall I suggest that the myth in fact tells truly of imaginative developments in the sixteenth and seventeenth centuries. Marshall McLuhan's *Gutenberg Galaxy* (London, Routledge and Kegan Paul, 1962) is an example of 'mythic history' and the difficulty of disentangling the two. Although his procedures and ambitions are very different from mine, at the centre of both stories is Renaissance man falling from sensuous harmony into visual obsession.

If Being and Appearance part company for ever, and this — as Marx once remarked — is indeed the basic assumption of all modern science, then there is nothing left to be taken upon faith; everything must be doubted.
After being and appearance had parted company and truth was no longer supposed to appear, to reveal and disclose itself to the mental eye of a beholder, there arose a veritable necessity to hunt for truth behind deceptive appearances . . . in order to be certain one had to *make sure*.[3]

From the mythic standpoint, what Descartes did for philosophy, Hamlet did for literature: 'Seems Madam? Nay, it is: I know not seems' (I. ii.). Innocence, in these terms, is believing that things are as they seem, or indeed not even raising the question. Fallen man is in doubt, and cannot accept and trust and expose himself to what he does not know; and it is for their radical rejection of the seeming world that Yeats singles out Hamlet and Descartes as typical modern men. Their historical task is to be seen not primarily in terms of right action, but rather in terms of exchanging doubts for certainties. In short, the myth we are dealing with here is the epistemological version of the Fall, a lucid summary of which is provided by Donne:

And new Philosophy calls all in doubt,
The element of fire is quite put out.
                                   ('The First Anniversary')

*

The modern figure emerging from our story is a solitary and embattled individual, surrounded by a world he does not trust; and his cognitive ambitions already look decidedly aggressive. Whether he be philosopher, scientist or lover, he will himself admit that he wants to make something of the world, not merely observe its passing. In the following pages I shall suggest that this figure may usefully be seen as a spider: that his desires to make something of the world

3. These two quotations are from pp. 250 and 263 of Hannah Arendt's *The Human Condition*. The sixth section of this book is devoted to an extensive discussion of the legacy of Cartesian doubt. Yeats makes the same point about seventeenth-century man with characteristic economy: 'A time had come when man must have certainty, and man knows what he has made. Man has made mathematics, but God reality' (E 435).

involve the distortion of its true nature; that his real aim is to feed the self at the expense of the other; and that such an aim is ultimately perverse, fantastic, and hence self-defeating.

Let us begin with the lover. In Donne's 'Twicknam Garden' we discover what happens when the courtier loses faith in his lady. Since for him she is no less than the world itself, his dilemma is truly metaphysical if she cannot be trusted:

> Alas, hearts do not in eyes shine,
> Nor can you more judge womans thoughts by teares,
> Than by her shadow, what she weares.

The elusiveness of her being calls forth 'the spider love', the poet's rage for complete knowledge and possession:

> Blasted with sighs, and surrounded with teares,
> Hither I come to seeke the spring,
> And at mine eyes, and at mine eares,
> Receive such balmes, as else cure every thing;
> But O, selfe traytor, I do bring
> The spider love, which transubstantiates all,
> And can convert Manna to gall,
> And that this place may thoroughly be thought
> True Paradise, I have the serpent brought.

The serpent he has brought is not only the forbidden knowledge that things are seldom what they seem, but also the instrument with which he would penetrate 'the other' to discover its real nature. Obsessed by the serpent, he cannot enjoy the spectacle of spring before his eyes because his false mistress has taught him to distrust their evidence. In the spider's eye the superficial delights of the garden are but grist for the mill of the mind, which would grasp their underlying essence. And just as the Christian bread and wine are changed from existing particulars into timeless universals, so the spider love is not content until it has penetrated the deceptive flesh, annihilated the accidents of time and place which are the root of all deception, and disclosed the immortal soul which it may embrace without fear. This kind of love 'can convert Manna to gall' not only because it may involve the destruction of the beloved, but also because it means more generally the loss of all innocent, non-aggressive relations with the inhabitants of the garden.[4]

In seventeenth-century England, the philosopher and the scientist were more significant figures than the lover in the determination of modern man's approach to the world. The classic description of their version of spider love is Jonathan Swift's story of the spider and the bee in *The Battle of the Books,* which Yeats lucidly summarizes thus: ' . . . or like the spider in Swift's parable mistake for great possessions what we spin out of our guts and deride the bee that has nothing but its hum and its wings, its wax and its honey, its sweetness and light' (EI 409). In this parable, Swift identifies himself with the ancients' bee and laments the modern mind's spidery approach to the world:

> For, upon the highest corner of a large window, there dwelt a certain spider, swollen up to the first magnitude by the destruction of infinite numbers of flies whose spoils lay scattered before the gates of his palace, like human bones before the cave of some giant . . .
>
> 'Not to disparage myself,' [said the spider to the bee] 'by the comparison with such a rascal, what art thou but a vagabond without house or home, without stock or inheritance, born to no possession of your own but a pair of wings and a drone-pipe? . . . Whereas I am a domestick animal, furnished with the native stock within myself. This large castle (to show my improvements in the mathematicks) is all built with my own hands, and the materials extracted altogether out of my own person.' . . .
>
> [The bee replies:] 'I visit indeed all the flowers and blossoms of the field and the garden; but whatever I collect from thence enriches myself, without the least injury to their

4. Spider love is also the principal theme of the *Winter's Tale,* which Leontes declares in a speech based on the contemporary superstition that spiders are only venomous if they are seen: 'I have drunk and seen the spider' (II.i.). In the preceding scene the spider's transubstantiating potential is registered:

> And all eyes
> Blind with the pin and web, but theirs: theirs only
> That would unseen be wicked? Is this nothing?
> Why, then the world and all that's in't is nothing,
> The covering sky is nothing, Bohemia nothing,
> My wife is nothing, nor nothing have these nothings
> If this be nothing.

The irony here is that both Leontes and Donne's lover are blinded by their insights.

beauty, their smell, or their taste... You boast, indeed, of being obliged to no other creature, but of drawing and spinning out all from yourself; that is to say, if we may judge of the liquor in the vessel by what issues out, you possess a good plentiful store of dirt and poison in your breast . . . Your inherent portion of dirt does not fail of acquisitions, by sweepings exhaled from below; and one insect furnishes you with the share of poison to destroy another. So that in short, the question comes all to this; which is the nobler being of the two, that which by a lazy contemplation of four inches round, by an overweening pride, feeding and engendering on itself, turns all into excrement and venom, producing nothing at last, but fly-bane and a cobweb; or that which, by an universal range, with long search, much study, true judgement, and distinction of things, brings home honey and wax.' [5]

The opposition between the spider and the bee can be construed in many ways; the spider for example is a marvellous image of the capitalist, and the 'lazy contemplation of four inches round' makes one think of Descartes' spidery retreat to a bed of doubt and mathematics. [6] But for present purposes, the distinction may be simply summarized. The bee touches lightly upon the surfaces of things and pollination is his parable of sexuality, an equitable exchange of pollen for nectar. [7] The spider on the contrary must penetrate

5. Jonathan Swift, *The Battle of the Books*, in *Works*, III, London, 1803, pp. 211-215.

6. Descartes found the only warrant for his existence in his own mental activity. The capitalist is a less subtle kind of 'self-made' man. Shakespeare sees Cardinal Wolsey, the butcher's son who acquired great wealth and power, as a spider:

> There's in him stuff that puts him to these ends:
> For being not propt up by ancestry, whose grace
> Chalks successors their way; nor called upon
> For high feats done to the crown; neither allied
> To eminent assistants; but spider-like
> Out of his self-drawing web.
>
> *(Henry VIII*, I. i.)

7. Yeats's 'great purple butterfly' bears a family resemblance:

> That is how he learnt so well
> To take the roses for his meat.
>
> (CP 192)

and possess. Not unlike idealist poets and philosophers, he catches existence on the wing and inters it in a fabric of his own devising, where it ceases to be itself (i.e. as it appears) and becomes a part of him (i.e. takes on his colouring). Though he might agree that his appetite is gross, he simply cannot find nourishment in the surfaces of things.

The defining characteristic of the spider is his disbelief in or disrespect for the otherness of the other. As the Swift passage indicates, however, confusion may arise regarding the kind of distortion he practises. Is he lazy and fat, too busy playing with himself to notice what goes on around him, or is he aggressive and shrewd, lying still and hidden but concentrating in the eye those talents which will *know* his victims utterly?

One might deal with this problem by referring to spiders as either web-spinners or fly-catchers; and yet Swift is surely right to resist such a rigid separation, for the similarities between the two activities are ultimately more important than the differences. Both fly-catching and web-spinning originate in doubt and the assumption of 'the other's' hostility (or at least intractability); and although the fly-catcher concentrates upon — while the web-spinner seems to ignore — 'the other', both are crucially ignorant of the harmonies Adam knows in the Garden, and the activity of both is an attempt to recover this loss; and even if one thinks of the fly-catcher as a menace and the web-spinner as a harmless fantasist, their different sorts of distortion may leave them equidistant from a true perception of the-self-in-the-other. But most importantly, the fly-catcher's aggression is psychologically implicit in the web-spinner's narcissism, and vice versa; as Swift indicates, the aggression is logically and psychologically prior to the narcissism, and the narcissist tends to deny or forget his aggressive relations with the world, a point we shall notice presently about Salome, who is the consummate expression of spideriness.

The unity-in-diversity of the spider's two functions is nicely illustrated in the comparison of Bacon's famous web-spinning Schoolmen with the fly-catching Scientific Rationalists whom Swift had in mind:

This kind of degenerate learning did chiefly reign among the schoolmen: who having sharp and strong wits, and abundance of leisure, and small variety of reading; but their wits being shut up in the cells of a few authors (chiefly Aristotle their dictator) as their persons were shut up in the cells of monasteries and colleges; and knowing little history, either of nature or time; did out of no great quantity of matter, and infinite agitation of wit, spin out unto us those laborious webs of learning which are extant in their books. *For the wit and mind of man, if it work upon matter, which is the contemplation of the creatures of God, worketh according to the stuff, and is limited thereby;* but if it work upon itself, as the spider worketh his web, then it is endless, and brings forth indeed cobwebs of learning, admirable for the fineness of thread and work, but of no substance or profit. [My italics.] [8]

The Schoolmen (not unlike the modern Symbolist poets) avoided Nature because they feared to meet the devil and their own limitations there. The Scientific Rationalists, whom we shall now consider, plundered Nature in the hope of becoming its Lord. The difference between the two, *sub specie aeternitatis*, is not that great.

*

One of the most significant acts of spidery destruction perpetrated by the new scientists was the astronomer's rending of the heavenly fabric; or so the poets would have us believe in any case.[9] What makes the astronomer such an appropriate target is that his mathematics arguably destroy

8. *The Advancement of Learning,* Book One. That Bacon can detect the spider in the Schoolmen aptly illustrates that the spider myth is not only applicable to imaginative developments in the Renaissance. This fact will embarrass only those who would unnecessarily confine the myth's range and see it as a dispensation revealed at a certain time in history. The spider is not so historically situated: as the Bacon passage demonstrates, he simply symbolizes certain kinds of corruption in the mind's relations to its objects; and though my concern here is with the Renaissance spider, there can be no objection to the search for a different species in another time and place.

the otherness of man's most ancient source of wonder. Donne expands his denunciation of the astronomer's spider in a marvellous passage:

> For of Meridians, and Parallels,
> Man hath weav'd out a net, and this net throwne
> Upon the Heavens, and now they are his owne.
> Loth to goe up the hill, or labour thus
> To goe to heaven, we make heaven come to us.
>   ('The First Anniversary', lines 279-83)

If one believes Hannah Arendt, these lines convey a remarkably accurate picture of the imaginative significance of the new science.[10]

9.   Miss Arendt agrees: ' . . . and the author of the decisive event of the modern age is Galileo rather than Descartes' (HC 248).

10.   Here are two passages from her *Human Condition* which suggestively describe the scientific spider:

> Cartesian reason is entirely based 'on the implicit assumption that the mind can only know that which it has itself produced and retains in some sense within itself' [Whitehead]. Its highest ideal must therefore be mathematical knowledge as the modern age understands it, that is, not the knowledge of ideal forms given outside the mind but of forms produced by a mind which in this particular instance does not even need the stimulation — or, rather, the irritation — of the senses by objects other than itself. This theory is certainly what Whitehead calls it, 'the outcome of common-sense in retreat'.
>
>   (p. 257)
>
> In other words the world of the experiment seems always capable of becoming a man-made reality, and this, while it may increase man's power of making and acting, even of creating a world, far beyond what any previous dared to imagine in dream and phantasy, unfortunately puts man back once more — and now even more forcefully — into the prison of his own mind, into the limitations of patterns he himself created. The moment he wants what all ages before him were capable of achieving, that is, to experience the reality of what he himself is not, he will find that nature and the universe 'escape him' and that a universe construed according to the behaviour of nature in the experiment and in accordance with the very principles which man can translate technically into a working reality lacks all possible representation.
>
>   (p. 261)

See Bertrand Russell's *Autobiography*, II, p. 158 for confirmation of this view.

Yeats, himself no philosopher, none the less had a shrewd idea where the battle lines were drawn: 'Descartes, Locke, and Newton took away the world and gave us its excrement instead. Berkeley restored the world' (E 325). The world Yeats has in mind here is the one we hold in common, full of colours, smells and birdsong; and what he found so attractive about Berkeley (apart from his Irishness) was his 'belief in perception' (EI 402), by virtue of which he excoriated the abstractions of the materialists. Because everything in the sensible world 'stands in God's unchanging eye' (CP 305), which subtends and guarantees its reality, there is no need for the scientific spider to probe its composition. Needless to say the spider's advance was not long arrested by Berkeley's defiant stand; but as in the case of Swift, Yeats was pleased that the chief evils of the modern age were best noticed, denounced and opposed in fine Anglo-Irish prose.

Donne's attack on the seventeenth-century astronomer announced a major theme of the modern age, the poet's critique of the scientist's hubris. Nowadays the arguments against the Faustian scientist have become so obvious, so ignored, and hence so unequivocally apocalyptic that cliché is difficult to avoid. These arguments were by no means so obvious when Yeats was a young man; but from the beginning he knew where his sympathies lay, and in the very first of his *Collected Poems* the evil astronomer is thus denounced:

> Seek, then,
> No learning from the starry men,
> Who follow with the optic glass
> The whirling ways of stars that pass —
> Seek, then, for this is also sooth,
> No word of theirs — the cold star-bane
> Has cloven and rent their hearts in twain,
> And dead is all their human truth.

Yeats's 'optic glass' provides a striking image of the spider's eye, which as a matter of fact is composed of several magnifying lenses. That this point is not altogether irrelevant to the present discussion is I hope evident in this fine passage from Ruskin:

Flowers, like everything else that is lovely in the visible
world, are only to be seen rightly with the eyes which the
God who made them gave us; and neither with microscopes
nor spectacles. These have their uses for the curious and
the aged; as stilts and crutches have for people who want
to walk in mud, or cannot safely walk but on three legs
anywhere. But in health of mind and body, men should
see with their own eyes, hear and speak without trumpets,
walk on their feet, not on wheels, and work and war with
their arms, not with engine-beams, nor rifles warranted to
kill twenty men at a shot before you can see them.[11]

In Ruskin's view the magnifying glass penetrates the God-
given integrity of the natural world and destroys the mystery
and the *haecceity* of its woven fabric, reverence for which is
one of man's most ancient and reliable ways of reminding
himself that he is not God. The implication here is that the
optic glass and the other 'extensions of man' made possible
by science and technology, are primarily machines of
aggression against the otherness of the other, the employment
of which also undermines the integrity of the self.[12] Although
the logic of this process is a complex one, no sane citizen
today can fail to perceive that Ruskin was right, particularly
since the hundred years between him and us have demonstrated

---

11.   *Ruskin Today,* ed. Kenneth Clark, p. 71.

12.   Marshall McLuhan agrees, or at least seems to, in his Chapter IV on
Narcissus as Narcosis in *Understanding Media: The Extensions of Man.*
(Sphere Books, London, 1967). Unlike Ruskin, however, he also seems
to believe that 'if the fool would persist in his folly he would become
wise', and that electronics are reconstituting Humpty Dumpty, at a higher
level of course. Those readers who find excessive the inclusion of spectacles
in Ruskin's inventory of aggressive instruments may be impressed by
Desmond Morris:

> A direct stare is typical of the most out-and-out aggression. It is part of
> the fiercest facial expressions and accompanies all of the most
> belligerent gestures . . . The wearing of spectacles and sun-glasses makes
> the face appear more aggressive because it artificially and accidentally
> enlarges the pattern of the stare. If we are looked at by someone
> wearing glasses, we are being given a super-stare. Mild-mannered
> individuals tend to select thin-rimmed or rimless spectacles (probably
> without realizing why they do so) because this enables them to see
> better with the minimum of stare exaggeration.
>
> (*The Naked Ape,* pp. 143-4)

so vividly how crippling technology can be in the hands of those whose 'knees no longer bend'.[13]

The difference between the scientist's and the poet's interest in the other has often been less than many poets (including Yeats) have liked to suppose; and hence one might expect that in an age when, as Hegel says, artists, too, find kneeling difficult, one will also find poets searching through the 'optic glass'. Most conveniently for my purposes, I find this nowhere more persuasively suggested than in Yeats's *Autobiographies:*

> [Dowson and Johnson] had taught me that violent energy, which is like a fire of straw, consumes in a few minutes the nervous vitality, and is useless in the arts. Our fire must burn slowly, and we must constantly turn away to think, constantly analyse what we have done, be content even to have little life outside our work, to show, perhaps, to other men, as little as the watch-mender shows, his magnifying-glass caught in his screwed-up eye. Only then do we learn to conserve our vitality, to keep our mind enough under control and to make our technique sufficiently flexible for expression of the emotions of life as they arise.
>
> (A 318)

In this portrait of the artist, Yeats depicts with uncanny accuracy the frightening ambiguities in the poetic posture he aspires to adopt. On the one hand, one can see in it the poet as hero, redeeming both self and other through sacrifice. By eschewing the active exploration of his own energies, by

13. The phrase is Hegel's, and it occurs in a passage suggesting that we should no longer look to art for the practice of reverence:

> One can indeed hope that art will go on developing and perfecting itself; nevertheless its form has ceased to be the highest need of the spirit. Whatever excellencies we may find in the statues of the Greek gods; whatever dignity and perfection we may see in the representations of God the Father, Christ and Mary — these cannot help us: for our knees no longer bend.
>
> (*Aesthetik*, p. 137)

Yeats agrees that reverence is not modern: 'My mediaeval knees lack health until they bend' (CP 369).

On the irreverence of twentieth-century man, and the scientist in particular, there can be little more to say. One who says it with admirable restraint is Gregory Bateson: see his 'Conscious Purpose Versus Nature' in *Dialectics of Liberation* (ed. David Cooper).

forfeiting his own beauty and all perfections of the life, indeed by hardly *mattering* at all, the poet hopes to give expression to 'the emotions of life as they arise', and so redeem the Minute Particulars he has lost. By finding himself in the play of others, he would extinguish, or rather transfigure, his own desires to take part.

On the other hand, if this heroic alchemy fails, as it must do when the community breaks down, the poet is clearly a spider. Far from selflessly conferring identity upon 'the emotions of life as they arise', he lies in wait and captures their reflections in his golden eye; ugly, sedentary and watchful, he vicariously dissects the life on which he feeds. In short, he is a voyeur; and his decision to 'conserve' his vitality leads not to the transfiguration of violent energy but to its repression, and eventually to an 'expression' arguably more aggressive than the layman's 'fire of straw' he initially rejects. Showing himself as little as possible, he is almost completely absorbed in the secret discipline which keeps his alchemical fires under sufficient pressure and his long legs sufficiently flexible that they may be equal to 'the emotions of life as they arise'.[14]

The watch-mender or the goldsmith with 'his magnifying glass caught in his screwed-up eye' is an ambiguous figure, for he looks myopic as well as acutely perceptive; and indeed this ambiguity is fundamental to the spider. We saw at the outset that Yeats took the Romans' drilled eyeball to represent a busy commerce between subject and object, but when he came to Hamlet, he emphasized not the look in his eye, but the rapier thrust in his fingers. Just as a blind person must 'see' with his hands, so Hamlet, mistrusting the appearances of things, must try to *grasp* their reality.[15] Again

14. Yeats was not insensitive to the evil potential in this image of the poetic posture. Referring to contemporary poetry, he speaks of a 'minute psychological curiosity, suggesting an eye where a goldsmith's magnifying glass is screwed . . .' (Introduction to *The Ten Principal Upanishads*, p. 10). Yeats is at some level registering the ambiguity here, for his goldsmiths originate in Byzantium, where at their best they hammer out golden solutions to the problems of existence. See CP 217. (Cf. also L 853.)

15. The groping hand appears several times in *The Tower* collection:

And should some crazy hand dare touch a daughter . . . (CP 237)

For every hand is lunatic/That travels on the moon. (CP 249)

And in *The Winding Stair*: 'We grope, and grope in vain, / For children born of her pain. / Children dazed and dead!' (CP 273)

in the Swift passage, the spider's eye looks outward only to catch his prey and is blind to the rich variety which delights the bee; indeed its confusion can become such that it narcissistically denies altogether the reality of the other and claims to have produced everything out of itself. In 'Twicknam Garden', the point is explicitly made that spider love is blinding the lover to the garden's delights; and in the *Winter's Tale*, Leontes is blinded when he sees the spider — a fine paradox.

As for Yeats's spidery eyesight, it was not just a question of Hamlet's legacy in the twentieth century; as Dorothy Wellesley observes, it had other sources as well:

> The matter of Yeats' visual life is deeply interesting. To an English poet it appears at times incredible . . . I have come to the conclusion that [his] lack of 'visualness', this lack of interest in natural beauty for its own sake, may originate in the fact that most of the Celtic poets are not concerned with nature at all . . . But of Yeats I think it is possible that to this racial characteristic must be added his extremely poor sight. His small dark eyes turned outwards, appear like those of a lizard and as though at times they were hidden by a film . . .
> how strongly Yeats disliked flowers, and how *his lack of observation concerning natural beauty was almost an active obsession* . . . [My italics.]
>
> (LDW 173)

*

Our story began when Adam lost touch with his body and hence with Nature herself; and we have considered various strategies devised by the individualist spider for the recovery of this loss. It has on the whole been a sad story, for the garden Adam left was a harmonious community and he has tried to return as its master: which is to forget the father.

But if Adam's imperial designs are misguided, as I have implied throughout, what should he be doing? Clearly once the apple has been eaten there can be no simple return to the *status quo ante bellum*; but there must be *some* alternative to the spider's assault, or else our disapproval of it lacks substance. In short, if we cannot indicate how Adam can at least lead a dignified existence in the shadow of his lost paradise, our myth is inadequate. The philosopher who has most profoundly addressed this problem in modern times is Hegel.

For our purposes, a crude outline of his historical myth will suffice. [16] He begins with Adam falling into knowledge and self-alienation (*Selbstentfremdung*): 'Knowledge, as the disannulling of the unity of mere Nature, is the "Fall", which is no casual conception, but the eternal history of Spirit.' [17] Mind, in other words, annuls that touch of Nature which makes the whole world kin, and Adam discovers his solitude. The discovery of otherness provokes the desire for its conquest, and the unity Adam seeks is not that of 'mere Nature' but a complex dialectical recognition of the self-in-the-other, in which the self at once appropriates the other and assents to its own finitude. As an intellectual capitalist or cognitive explorer Adam plants himself in the other, thereby initiating the process through which he will subdue the earth and ultimately be gathered to it. For Hegel, however, the mastery and the submission are not two discrete processes, but the two aspects of *the* dialectical process. In religious terms the injunction is to 'Remember now thy Creator in the days of thy youth'.

Religious terms are by no means inapposite to Hegel's story; indeed one could argue that his ultimate intention was to recast the Christian problematic of pride and humility in forms which might nourish the increasingly secular imagination of the European Enlightenment. Adam was hungry for conquest and self-aggrandizement, and what he needed was a story that would sanction his aggressive desires by grounding them in a countervailing recognition of his own limitations — and of course the less such recognition restricted his acquisitive activities the better. Hegel certainly wrote vigorously of cognitive empires — the *Phenomenology,* for example, is full of ingestive imagery; whether he also wrote meaningfully of humility is far from certain. [18]

16. Or rather one version of his historical myth, for there are at least two. In the *Phenomenology* for example, it could be argued that Adam appropriates and then discards his estates one by one; i.e., that the emphasis is on the moving spirit of negation rather than on linear accumulation. In other words, Adam has them only by renouncing them.

17. Hegel, *Philosophy of History* (trans. Sibree), p. 321.

18. That Hegel's myth of Adam in aggressive pursuit of certain knowledge is representative of Enlightenment man is suggested in this description of the

In any case, Hegel's Adam is passionate for knowledge, and the process whereby he acquires it may most easily be understood in the relationship of two people. [19] Adam's cognitive exploration of an other, like most colonizing gestures, must have an aggressive moment, for the otherness of the other must in some sense be broken down before it can be appropriated; indeed the cognitive act bears formal comparison with the sexual act, for to know an other, to make it one's own, one must penetrate its opaque surface and grasp the principle of its being. But the process works both ways, as the known invades the knower; for in order to take the other in, the self must itself be taken, as the wax takes the impress of the seal. In human relations, both parties may emerge from the dialectical process whereby they appropriate and are appropriated (*aufgehoben*) by each other with a fuller sense of themselves, each finding in the other's eye a reflecting otherness in which its own boundaries are drawn. Thus both parties seek themselves in each other; and if they can correctly find reality and justice in becoming for themselves what they are to each other, then the voyage of mutual self-exploration establishes unpoliced frontiers, not exploitation. [20]   But when the integrities of either party are abused, the possibilities for spoliation in both cognitive and sexual relations are enormous.

---

philosophes by Peter Gay: ' . . . the energy that animated them was a drive for knowledge and control, a restless Faustian dissatisfaction with mere surfaces . . . The most popular metaphors of their writings were not merely metaphors of battle, but metaphors of penetration . . .' (*The Party of Humanity*, p. 43).

By the end of the nineteenth century those metaphors had not faded: 'The so-called thirst for knowledge may be traced to the lust of appropriation and of conquest' (Nietzsche, *Will to Power*).

19.   One might suspect that to take interpersonal relations as the paradigm of all relations between self and other is to overrate objects and underrate people. Not so: and one might think this only because our relations with objects have themselves become so degraded in the present age of throw-away items. In a world allowed to be alive, *all* transactions between self and other are lively ones, and the humblest of artefacts has an integrity which its users can know only through respectful submission. On the deadliness of modern man's relations with objects, see Benjamin's essay on Baudelaire in his *Illuminations*.

20.   See Hegel's *Phenomenology*, pp. 228-40.

The analogy between carnal knowledge and the sort which manifests itself in propositions is not merely fortuitous. The philosopher seeking certain knowledge of the other and the lover wanting to make sure of his beloved's devotion are both worried by the possibility that the other may indeed be radically and humiliatingly other. Both can be seen as banished from a garden in which lively relations obtain between subject and object, in which the other returns the gaze the self bestows upon it; and if their perplexity becomes extreme, both will consider murder as a logical conclusion to their search for certainty and possession. In terms of the myth, philosopher and lover are in similar situations, and this similarity is much more important than the fact that the lover attempts to seize the world in his beloved whereas the philosopher tries to take it as such.

If Adam's explorations prove successful, however, he will conclude with the ironic perception that he both possesses the other and does not; that is to say, he will realize himself as a creature who both is bounded in a particular space and time and yet also possesses a boundless capacity to occupy other forms. Indeed his unbounded self is free to range over nature and history, and as long as these expeditions are grounded in the contrary awareness of his own finitude, neither reality nor justice is violated. If they are not so grounded, however, the violation is profound. Instead of the imaginative occupation of other forms of space and time we find only a fantastic raid upon them, in which Adam not only mis-takes *their* nature but also mistakes for godlike metamorphosis in himself what is nothing more than narcissism.

As I said, it is by no means certain that Hegel's writings adequately convey the sorts of limitations in which Adam's cognitive activities must be grounded if they are to prosper. What *is* certain is that whatever humility his philosophy does commend did not take root in the Romantic imagination. Its failure to do so is declared and explored in Goethe's *Faust*, a work which William James recognized as the poetic analogue of Hegel's philosophy, and which can still tell us a great deal about the myth of modern man. The play opens with the scholarly Faust unsatisfied by a merely intellectual grasp of the world, and his thoughts turn to alchemy, the sort of word-magic shunned by the exponents of Enlightenment Rationalism. His desire to master everything ('der ganzen Menschheit') leads the wise Mephisto to call him 'Herr

Mikrokosmos' and point out that 'the single whole was fashioned for a god alone'. Mephisto recognizes in Faust the makings of a Romantic poet, and tries to restrain him with the reminder that however he may try to stalk about on fancy stilts ('ellenhohe Socken') he will always be what he is, a mortal man ('Du bleibst doch immer was du bist'); [21] indeed the only certain cure for his Romantic disease is to renounce ('entbehren') his vast hungers and confine himself in a limited sphere ('einem ganz beschränkten Kreise'), dig the land and tend his animals. But such radical therapy makes no sense to a man bent on self-aggrandizement and the desecration of nature; and so the mad pact is sealed, Faust's confusion settled.

The rest of the play leads Faust through the various forms of spidery delusion; as poet-historian he giddily ransacks the past, as lover he penetrates and destroys the surfaces of Gretchen's world, and at the end he is settling into the form of spidery restlessness most satisfying to nineteenth- and twentieth-century man, the union of capitalism and technology. As he absent-mindedly abolishes the old peasants and the last remnants of a pious way of life, he mouths nonsense about making the world safe for technological progress; and thus the stage is set for those 'rugged individualists' who have since Goethe's time redrawn the maps of the world to such devastating effect that Yeats, in a mood of sane and savage fury, could 'wonder what was left for massacre to save' (CP 383).

Goethe was too intelligent an artist to think that his monstrous conception might be damned; indeed the disturbing point of the play is that Faustian energies are modern energies, and western culture had even by 1800 exhausted the reserves of piety which alone could enable it to resist this hero. One may certainly notice that Goethe went too far in awarding eternal life to a man who did not even repent at the end. But argument about such failures of judgement in this work of genius are in danger of missing the important point: which is that it would be frivolous not to see in *Faust* a momentous recognition of modern man's failure to find secular ground in which the spirit of humility, hitherto nurtured by Christianity, might be rooted. As such it does not augur well for Yeats, who

21.   See especially lines 1730-1830.

in the poems we shall presently consider, is searching for
some ground on which he might be at home, hoping to
contain thereby the unreality that breeds in the alchemical
mind:

Hands, do what you're bid:
Bring the balloon of the mind
That bellies and drags in the wind
Into its narrow shed.

(CP 175)

*

As we observed earlier, spideriness is not an exclusively modern
affliction, but arises wherever contemplative word-magic goes
wrong, i.e. distorts its materials and ultimately mistakes its
mental reproduction of reality for the thing itself. The burden
of this chapter's argument has been to suggest that modern
man practises such magic extensively, and in ways that are
very liable to go wrong.

By the end of the nineteenth century a great deal of
spidery culture had accumulated: in science, in philosophy,
and in literature. Many intelligent men, notably the French
Symbolists, found this inheritance so deadening and oppress-
ive that there was no question of resuscitation; it had to be
rejected, abolished, destroyed. That is to say, the mental
culture of modern man, the culture based on *knowing*, was
so corrupted by spidery distortion that it was not possible to
correct its errors. The magic had gone bad, and instead of
putting man in touch with the sources of life it had decisively
hidden them from him.

The elimination of such deeply entrenched cultural practices
was a vast undertaking, and even today it has by no means
been accomplished. As they saw it the man of words, of
knowledge, whose eyes are directed aggressively towards the
world, must be abolished. In his place they put a beautiful
girl, a dancer whose empty eyes declare a blessedly ignorant
indifference to the world around her. The girl's name is
Salome, and the thoughtful man she replaces as culture-hero
is represented by the head of John the Baptist.

The complex history of Salome as a dominant influence on
the late nineteenth-century Decadents has been exhaustively

traced by Mario Praz in *The Romantic Agony* and its implications for Yeats suggestively discussed by Professor Kermode in *The Romantic Image*.[22] Although Yeats was fascinated by this figure from the nineties onwards, he was by no means altogether willing to endorse such a radical attack upon the past; for we must remember that the bulk of his poetry attempts to outwit the spider through a 'correct' practice of contemplative word-magic.[23]   But when he was thinking apocalyptic thoughts about the necessary destruction of European culture, he could appreciate the timeliness of Salome and the need to worship her:

> When I think of the moment before revelation I think of Salome — she, too, delicately tinted or maybe mahogany dark — dancing before Herod and receiving the Prophet's head in her indifferent hands, and wonder if what seems to us decadence was not in reality the exaltation of the muscular flesh and of civilisation perfectly achieved.
>
> (AV 273)

On this view Salome's beauty represents a healthy culture — 'where body is not bruised to pleasure soul' — culture unimpressed by the Christian spirituality which had come to infect it. She neither hates nor fears the *logos* of St John, but simply refutes it in the movements of her body. Seen in this way she may be the perfect antidote to Hamlet and the spider. The 'agile rapier and dagger' thrust between his fingers, which turned into 'slender needles of bone', have been replaced by 'indifferent hands', uninterested in what they hold; and the piercing look of the intellectual spider has yielded to empty eyes, reminiscent of the 'vague Grecian eyes gazing at nothing' (AV 277) which Yeats associated with self-possession; indeed, like many another sphinx the secret of Salome's mystery is that she has none.[24]

22.   See especially pp. 57-82.

23.   See above on his differences with Mallarmé, p. 29 ff.

24.   As Kermode points out, Flaubert's Salome 'forgets the name of the man whose head she is dancing for' (RI 74). He makes it clear that it was upon her vacant expression that the Decadents focused their admiration and worship.

One might call this the high-minded, abstract, hieratic and sexless view of Salome; and as such Yeats naturally found it congenial. There is another view, however, which begins much less abstractly, with Salome as a nineteenth-century decadent, closer to the Great Whore of Babylon than to a muscular 'civilisation perfectly achieved'. Her eyes are vacant not because they have no need to prey upon the world, but because they have been blinded to it by a narcissism incapable of taking it on. She needs nourishment as much as Hamlet ever did, but she is childlike in her ignorance of the world, and like a child simply expects to be fed. And she *is* fed; not because her innocence calls for protection, but because her mindless beauty is so composed as to appeal to the self-destructive instincts of her victims, the last weary exponents of a spidery culture. Herself the last product of this culture, she is the almost mechanical Black Widow in whom the others may die.[25]

Whichever view of Salome one takes, she is mythically related to the ancient Greek Maenads and other chthonic ladies who have traditionally dismembered poets for trying to enlarge upon the basic topics of birth and copulation and death. Yeats could take the first view of her when he was securely ensconced in his tower, perusing the maps of history, and hoping in Nietzschean fashion that twentieth-century apocalypse would bring forth a new muscular civilization in which the body would be free from the infection of modern spirituality. In a late play for example, an old man who gravely announces 'there must be severed heads' makes it clear which Salome he has in mind by adding 'I am old, I belong to mythology' (CPL 694). But Yeats was also capable of presenting the second view. In *The King's Threshold*, for instance, the nasty Salome appears in the guise of lovely princesses who come to seduce the poet. Their eyes seem innocuous, but he doubts their hands:

You've eyes of dancers; but hold out your hands,
For it may be there are none sound among you.

(CPL 132)

25. I call Salome 'almost mechanical', because she appears so uninterested in the severed head and the dance that requires it. This mechanical aspect was important to the Decadents, who located it in the 'dead face' she usually wore. There were exceptions, however, such as Evan John, who has her grinding the severed head between her thighs (RI 74).

On closer inspection, their limpid aristocratic hands reveal traces of leprosy, an appropriately grim conclusion to the story that began with Hamlet's 'agile rapier'.

Rather like Nietzsche, Yeats vacillated between the two versions of twentieth-century cataclysm which Salome can authorize. Although there was good reason to praise her muscular dancing, there was also plenty of evidence around that her decadent self offered no salvation but only dissolution and despair. For proof of this Yeats could look to France; but nearer home were his old friends, Dowson and Johnson, two of her finer victims. Unlike them, Yeats always kept her at a certain distance, and one might suggest, that he was too cautious, timid and uptight ever to put himself on the line and really take the conclusions of modern art seriously. On the other hand one could argue that he sanely resisted the extremes of Symbolism and, like Nietzsche, was ultimately bound to an ancient muse who told him that there can indeed be 'passion that has more life in it than death' (CP 115) and that in the twentieth century it is called irony.

On this view the ironist's responsibility is to register the collapse of culture without himself collapsing, and he does this by *understanding* how such a process is necessary and just. If he can do this without falling into spidery error, he may find a magical liveliness in the death that he contemplates. Such a figure, as we have seen, is a special kind of historian. If he is also a lyric poet, as Yeats was, he will have domestic stories to tell, about his own attempts to occupy a particular house in a particular landscape. Given the foul weather of the time, these stories will also be sad, but if one's memory is alive, there are household gods to invoke for counsel and benediction. If they are invoked with care and piety, one's own failures may also be seen as necessary and just, and hence forgiven. To these stories I shall now turn.

TOWER POEMS

> Thou look'st through spectacles; small things seeme great
> Below; But up unto the watch-towre get,
> And see all things despoyl'd of fallacies.
>
> (John Donne)

'Meditation in Time of Civil War' (1922)

Throughout most of these 'Meditations', Yeats is pondering
the tower, the possibility of his being at home there, and of
having parental relations with his surroundings. If he cannot
mother Ireland, what can he do for his own children? If he
cannot plant real flowers, may he still fashion the 'symbolic
rose' (CP 226)? Would such a rose indicate anything but its
own impossibility? And is the alchemist who works upon it
bearing witness to a barren age or only hiding himself away?
He couldn't ask more searching questions, and on no other
occasion asks them better.

I 'Ancestral Houses'

This poem was written one year before the others in this
sequence, and is different in setting, style and mood. It is also
inferior. I therefore propose to ignore it.

II 'My House'

> Surely a man shall see the noblest works and foundations
> have proceded from childless men.[1]

In this poem, nature is bleak and unfruitful, even menacing.
In such ground life cannot be planted. As Yeats says in
'My Descendants':

> and yet it seems
> Life scarce can cast a fragrance on the wind,
> Scarce spread a glory to the morning beams,
> But the torn petals strew the garden plot.

In view of these conditions, one must cultivate the soul's
'symbolic rose', not the real one. The exposure and risk

1. Francis Bacon, 'Parents and Children'.

involved in begetting new life are such that one's energies are better spent in an effort to get wisdom and understanding.

Instead of sunlight then, 'A candle and written page', by which imagination can illuminate the Forms themselves, not their pale shadows disclosed by the soul's 'natural declension' in the sun. The poet compares himself to Milton's monkish *penseroso* who chose to live with 'divinest Melancholy', that 'sad virgin', asking her to 'Hide me from Day's garish eie':

> And when the sun begins to fling
> His flaring beams, me Goddes bring
> To arched walks of twilight groves.

Since Yeats calls *il penseroso* a Platonist, it is worth mentioning the *Symposium,* which culminates in Socrates's famous discourse on love as the search for immortality through the creation of Beauty. According to Socrates, the begetting of children is the most rudimentary form this search can take. Considerably more enlightened than this is the begetting of spiritual children, such as Homer's poems. True immortality however is attained only by the philosopher in contemplative conjunction with 'sole and absolute Beauty'.

Upon such spiritual rock Yeats has founded his house. His 'symbolic rose', unmoved by wind and weather, towers above the 'benighted travellers', emblematic perhaps of a disinherited generation who

> ... shift about — all that great glory spent —
> Like some poor Arab tribesman and his tent.

> (CP 276)

To shift about may be one authentic response to an age of dispossession, and Yeats knows something of its barrenness. To occupy an ancestral house, on the other hand, such as the ones lamented in the previous poem, would be an absurdly anachronistic undertaking. But to find himself in a tower such as this one may be perfectly appropriate, for it both enables him to explore the implications of dispossession and yet it also provides him with some ground, without which not even 'the symbolic rose can break into flower'.

Just as the man-at-arms founded himself upon the impossibility of casting his blood into worldly forms (an image which anticipates 'The Black Tower') Yeats has founded himself upon the impossibility of casting his emblems in forms that will nourish his society's life. And yet Yeats's defiant renunciation differs from that of the master-at-arms and Milton's *penseroso* in one crucial respect. Although his poems and his house compose 'befitting emblems of adversity', he has contradicted (even perhaps betrayed) the purity of his line by founding a family. Are not the responsibilities of a father incompatible with those of a poet perceiving reality and justice in 'stony ground'? One wonders, for example, if a man can honestly write in 'Prayer for My Daughter' about the inevitable and ultimately justified destruction of ancestral houses while hoping that his daughter's bridegroom may

> bring her to a house
> Where all's accustomed, ceremonious.

(CP 214)

Such questions as these are surely relevant to the composition of a poem about 'My House'; but the only indication that Yeats is not alone in the tower comes at the end, where some impressively subtle syntax manages to suggest both that he has 'founded here' *for* his bodily heirs, and also that he is leaving them such emblems of adversity as the tower and this poem, which 'exalt a lonely mind': his certainly, theirs if they can match it. The ambiguity is masterful, but the fundamental problems have not really been confronted, let alone resolved.

III 'My Table'

In this meditation Yeats sits staring at the poems he cannot write, and looks to an old Japanese sword on the table for inspiration. It symbolizes for him not so much the warrior virtues of the Samurai as the five hundred years of high culture those virtues sustained. Placed between two poems which lament the breaking of the western tradition, and more specifically, Yeats's anxiety about what he can pass on to his children, the sword makes its point with chilling simplicity.

But it makes another point as well. The sword is simple and strong and deadly: above all it is unequivocal. It declares without a trace of rhetoric, embellishment or deceptiveness, exactly what it is and what it does. Unlike the poet's pen it lies beside, it never masks its wounding function. More generally, it is an almost universal symbol of man's questing spirit; and in a later poem the same sword appears in such a role, as an object 'Emblematical of love and war' (CP 265). (See L 729.) In sum, it represents with perfect clarity an eternal truth about human life, and it is this 'changeless' clarity that Yeats is admiring here. In its presence his poems remain unwritten because he can find nothing to say worthy of the example it sets. Rather than lower his standards and jeopardize his immortal soul, he chooses to remain silent — the poem says virtually nothing about Yeats or Ireland or his house or even his table — and console himself with the story of a Japanese gentleman.

This story is consoling not only because it distracts Yeats from his Irish depression, but more importantly because it suggests that what really counts is not one's worldly accomplishments nor the degree of culture one's family may enjoy, but the 'aching' perception that they will in any case fall far short of perfection. The Japanese gentleman, though possessed of the sword, 'silken clothes and stately walk', none the less 'had such an aching heart'; and we are invited to infer that such idealism is what the sword ultimately represents.

Yeats recognizes that in the light of the sword's noble tradition he has nothing to say, nor any cultural possessions to speak of; but this, far from disqualifying him from the fine company of those who have, only proves that he too has 'waking wits', and hence is entitled to keep the Japanese sword on his table.

It is one of the most subtle poems he ever wrote, full of Symbolist magic, 'beauty born out of its own despair' (CP 245). Beginning in speechless depression, it points to the sword as a good reason for keeping silent. By the end of the poem, the silence has been kept — the poem as advertised, about 'My Table', has not been written — and yet out of that silence a convincingly beautiful despair has been uttered. By exploring the conditions of its own impossibility the poem brings itself to life, in eloquent testimony to the poet's belief that

> only an aching heart
> Conceives a changeless work of art.

IV 'My Descendants'

Can one father children as well as poems? In this meditation the problem that disturbs the conclusion of 'My House' is faced more directly. The conflict between natural and spiritual children is at least as old as Plato's *Symposium*. Yeats once said that he had seen more artists ruined by wives and children than by harlots (A 484); and Blake, one of his chief mentors, 'felt that the family was the main breach in the visionary's defences through which all the powers of compromise come pouring with their threats and their wheedling'.[2]

Yeats has inherited a vigorous mind from his 'old fathers' and seems uncertain as to whether his true progeny are 'a woman and a man' he leaves behind or the dreams he has nourished. This problem does not of course arise for those whose vigour resides in the blood:

> 'Whatever stands in field or flood,
> Bird, beast, fish or man,
> Mare or stallion, cock or hen,
> Stands in God's unchanging eye
> In all the vigour of its blood;
> In that faith I live or die.'
>
> (CP 305)

Yeats would be the first to admit that unlike the violent bitter men who were his ancestors, he does not stand open and confident in the vigour of his blood. Since he does not stand thus in God's unchanging eye, he must use what he has, a vigorous mind, to build a foundation, a being, of comparable — perhaps even superior — dignity and durability.

This argument (which we shall meet again in 'Blood and the Moon') is of central importance to Yeats: if one cannot have substantial power, should one not be absolute for knowledge? In an earlier poem addressed to his 'old fathers', he seemed worried that his knowledge was not worthy of their power: that his words alone might not suffice to establish the substantial continuity of their line:

> Pardon that for a barren passion's sake,
> Although I have come close on forty-nine,
> I have no child, I have nothing but a book,
> Nothing but that to prove your blood and mine.   (CP 113)

2. Northrop Frye, *Fearful Symmetry*, p. 352.

Since that time, whether to hedge his bets or in response to circumstances beyond his control, he has taken on house, wife and children. No longer sharing the problematic purity of *il penseroso*'s renunciation, he has invested himself to some extent in the realm of blood. Explicitly dubious about his ability and/or inclination to edify his own children, he may well be all the more sceptical about the possibility of his writing poems which will help the Irish 'fill the cradles right' (CP 399) — in which case everything depends on his 'symbolic rose', which, if not a *fleur du mal*, is certainly *symboliste*, planted in poetry's power to *nier les choses*, growing from the negations of the actual.

The first four lines masterfully present his perplexity. They can be read as the words of a man who, because of time and circumstance, has been forced to nourish dreams instead of waking thoughts; and hence he is grateful that he has also produced 'a woman and a man . . . as vigorous of mind' to preserve the line and perhaps in less troubled times do justice to the inheritance of mind. And yet one also finds the very opposite sense in these lines. In view of his inheritance, his first responsibility has been the nourishment of dreams. Compared with this activity (which is placed right next to 'my old fathers') the treatment of his children is remarkably diffident. The third line has no pronouns, no possessives; instead of my children (aged one and three years at the time) we find 'a woman and a man'. Not only this, but the rhythm and line are such that one reads 'I must nourish dreams and leave a woman and a man behind'. To this statement 'as vigorous of mind' seems to be tacked on as an afterthought, a compensation both for them and for him: for them in that, if he has to ignore them for his dreams, he has at least provided them with as good a genetic inheritance as his own; and for him in that, as the next lines indicate, though they may be destined for 'common greenness', he has done his best for them genetically speaking, and for all that, they *may* preserve the vigour of the Yeatsian mind.[3]

His reluctance to name his children seems all the more significant when one remembers that in Yeats's view the epic poet's essential function is to name, to confer identity upon a society which without his shaping spirit can be but a

3. Yeats's daughter Anne is quoted (by Virginia Moore in *The Unicorn*, p. 337) as having said 'It must be nice to have two parents'.

collection of orphans. We have already noticed Yeats attempting this in 'Easter 1916' ('our part but to murmur name upon name') and it may also be the allegorical concern of 'Two Songs of a Fool', which ends with the beautifully simple suggestion that naming is the first and last parental function, and that children uncalled may wander into the night:

> Had I but awakened from sleep
> And called her name, she had heard,
> It may be, and had not stirred,
> That now, it may be, has found
> The horn's sweet note and the tooth of the hound.
>
> (CP 191)

The suggestion in both poems that the little ones die for lack of naming, and that their deaths may be sweet — to them and/ or to us — uncovers one of the most profound ambiguities by which the modern imagination is bewildered.[4]

As a poet with epic aspiration in an evil age, Yeats has registered dead children; and this may not be irrelevant to his calling in the second stanza of 'My Descendants' for no more marriages. What immediately appalls him is the prospect of his being known in and through the future inhabitants of Thoor Ballylee. If, as he thinks likely, his descendants smudge the clear outline of the symbolic flower to which his essential energies have been committed, he prays that the tower may remain faithful to the Yeatsian spirit and erase the evidence of his having engrossed himself in a family way; and thereby proclaim through the stones which are 'my symbol' (CP 268) the uncompromising dedication of his life and work to excellence.[5]

Stone ruins have been cherished by many sorts of Romantics as symbols of past glories and their present impossibility, or simply of the mutability of things. In a work of man being converted back into a work of Nature, one can see a nice

---

4. Yeats faces it again, more directly, a year after these 'Meditations':

> We grope, and grope in vain,
> For children born of her pain.
> Children dazed or dead!
>
> (CP 273)

His most searching exploration of child murder is in *Purgatory*, which is discussed in Chapter 5.

5. Cf.   And I am in despair that time may bring

reversal, indeed refutation, of the poetic imagination's pretensions to subdue the earth. Such atavism seldom fails to produce a *frisson*, though in the twentieth century we have arguably come to know it rather too well. In any case, in such ruinous rock the knowing and nocturnal owl may fittingly build and perhaps cry her envy of the swan which Yeats will by then have become, having leapt once and for all into 'the desolate heaven'.[6]

Yeats may have been shocked by the violence of this stanza. In any case his conclusion makes no mention of the tension between poetry and children, but rather concentrates upon the two women for whose friendship and love he has settled in this house. As if to say 'I am not all stone', he here admits a measure of implication in the flesh of woman. He needs and wants them, and because of this has made certain commitments to time and place:

> And know whatever flourish and decline
> These stones remain their monument and mine.

One thinks of the similar conclusion to 'The Municipal Gallery Revisited', a poem in which he is also searching for his ground:

> You that would judge me, do not judge alone
> This book or that, come to this hallowed place . . .
> Think where man's glory most begins and ends,
> And say my glory was I had such friends.

(CP 370)

'By their fruits ye shall know them.' Children are frightening enough to any parent who sees in them extensions of himself which he cannot control and yet by which he will be known and judged. In an age in which the falcon cannot hear the falconer, the control is that much less and the fright that much more. For a poet accustomed to absolute obedience from the images in which he finds himself, children must be a rather more harrowing experience than for mortals who live without the illusion of such mastery. And finally, for a poet who has attempted to generate himself out of the impossibility

> Approved patterns of women or of men
> But not that selfsame excellence again.   (CP 369)

6. Yeats's owl is not unrelated to Hegel's philosophical owl who spreads her wings at dusk.

of life's spreading its 'glory to the morning beams', the presence of Anne and Michael thumping about the tower in all their matter of fact must have seemed something perilously like self-contradiction, or at least self-parody.

V 'The Road at My Door'

This meditation opens with uncharacteristic simplicity, a vivid description of a man Yeats sees from his doorway one morning. In the second stanza the poet is introduced:

> A brown Lieutenant and his men,
> Half dressed in national uniform,
> Stand at my door, and I complain
> Of the foul weather, hail and rain,
> A pear-tree broken by the storm.

What is remarkable here is not just that the hail and rain and broken pear-tree are simply themselves and carry no symbolic freight, but that through them Yeats reveals himself — an existing individual who does not know what to make of the other which stands at his door. The inscrutability of these men is nicely suggested by 'A brown Lieutenant' and by their being 'half dressed' — should he invite them in? At a loss for words to place them in the web of his world-historical thought, he speaks of the weather (the breaking of a pear-tree, not western civilization) and they remain at the door, what they are, unassimilable others whose silence perhaps questions the authority of the words he writes when the door is closed.

But the door is closed; he can neither invite them in nor go out and join them. He returns to his chamber, pondering with envy the difference between their play in the sun and his barren imprisonment in the tower. Not even the contemplation of Nature's indifference to the absurd drama in her midst can relieve him, 'caught in the cold snows of a dream'.

VI 'The Stare's Nest by My Window'

In a passage describing the genesis of this poem Yeats wrote:

> Men must have lived so [i.e. violently] through many tumultuous centuries. One felt an overmastering desire not to ... lose all sense of the beauty of nature. A stare (our name for a starling) had built in a hole beside my window

and I made these verses out of the feeling of the moment
. . . Presently a strange thing happened. I began to smell
honey in places where honey could not be . . .

(A 580)

With no knowledge of this passage one tends to assume that
the mother bird in this poem has abandoned her nest (or
perhaps removed it to a more remote location) as a fitting
response from Nature to the dislocations in the body politic.
On the contrary, however, the above passage suggests that it
was the stare's *building* in Yeats's loosening wall which
cheered his gloomy contemplation of the surrounding devasta-
tion. And yet in the poem there can be little doubt that the
stare's house is empty.

The explanation is to be found in the honey-bees, which
in the prose passage are alchemical or mystic presences, not
actual insects. Thus the nest-building stare was an exoteric
manifestation, and the smelling of the alchemical honey its
esoteric counterpart. In transposing this experience into
poetry, Yeats empties the nest in order to symbolize his own
and Ireland's devastation, and invokes the honey-bees (quite
solid poetical honey-bees) to represent the hope for re-birth.

At the simplest level the poem seems to be asking, much in
the spirit of Swift's tale, that the present violence between
self and other might be replaced by the kind of life-enhancing
contact suggested by the honey-bee's exchange of pollen for
nectar. As a localized statement, asking that calm may succeed
the storm, it seems unexceptionable if somewhat common-
place. But though Yeats begins with his own tower and his
own wall, that wall is clearly metaphorical, and by the last
stanza he is speaking of 'We' Irish. Since the particulars are
generalized to this extent, one is forced to ask whether this
poem postulates (as Yeats frequently does in his prose) some
causal connection between violence and sweetness in Ireland.

In the biblical story (which Yeats explicitly invokes in
'Vacillation'), bees nested in the carcass of the lion dis-
membered by Samson, and 'Out of the eater came forth meat,
and out of the strong came forth sweetness' (Judges 14:14).
In a sense, the lion's destructive self is transformed through
death into a life-giving sweetness. May one then legitimately
infer that this poem is hoping for Yeats's and Ireland's
analogous transformation through the violence which has, in
a sense, entombed him in the tower?

The answer to this is probably yes, even though Yeats knows how deep the infection runs, as the last stanza indicates:

> We had fed the heart on fantasies,
> The heart's grown brutal from the fare;
> More substance in our enmities
> Than in our love; O honey-bees,
> Come build in the empty house of the stare.

In short, negation which is not itself overcome in subsequent affirmation breeds a brutalized fantasy, not new life. Yeats believed that Irish hatred was congenital:

> Out of Ireland have we come.
> Great hatred, little room,
> Maimed us at the start.
> I carry from my mother's womb
> A fanatic heart.[7]

(CP 288)

If the Irish have been maimed by hatred, castrated even, in what sense can they be restored by its exhaustion? Is it plausible to suggest (however tentatively) that a brutalized masculinity of guns and towers might give way to a receptive femininity of honey and loosening walls? Such transformation has certainly been an important theme in twentieth-century literature,[8] and though Yeats does not usually emphasize the sexual aspect, he knows the dialectic: '. . . original virtue arises from the discovery of evil. If we were, as I had dreaded . . . bitter beyond all the people of the world, we might yet lie . . . nearest the honeyed comb' (A 207). As one gathers from 'Ancestral Houses', sweetness and bitterness are dialectically conjoined, and the extremely sweet arises from the extremely bitter. But the bitterness and violence that builds great houses is so unlike that which literally dismembers 'the young soldier in his blood' that

---

7. Cf. 'The root of it all is that the political class in Ireland — the lower-middle class from whom the patriotic associations have drawn their journalists and their leaders for the last ten years — have suffered through the cultivation of hatred as the one energy of their movement, a deprivation which is the intellectual equivalent to a certain surgical operation' (A 486).

8. One thinks, e.g., of the castration of Joe Christmas in Faulkner's *Light in August*, and of Lawrence's *Women in Love*.

different terms really ought to be used; and whereas the dialectical logic in 'Ancestral Houses' is of a fairly conventional and unprovocative sort, in this case it appears more extreme and more dubious. It should be emphasized that this poem nowhere explicitly claims that violence generates honeybees; but in so far as it may be taken to imply some connection between the soldier's blood and a new fertility, it embodies a late Romanticism which I think one should resist.[9]

Suppose, however, we begin with diction and syntax, and ignore the problematic connections between violence and sweetness in Ireland. The poem at once appears more impressive. Short syntactic units, themselves not wholly explicit, are abruptly juxtaposed. No narrative line informs an ordered flow, no complex intelligence mediates the union of particular and universal. The diction throughout is both strikingly literal and colloquial. The over-all impression, paradoxically, is of simple and/or stark realities emerging from a context in which there is 'no clear fact to be discerned'. Here surely, as in the preceding meditation, is a fine example of what Auerbach discusses as the 'paratactic' style.[10] The unperiodic nature of parataxis indicates an inability or disinclination to organize connectedly a complex of information; and yet its directness and simplicity make possible the vivid expression of discrete events and intense feeling.

Seen as a comment upon his language, and implicitly therefore his state of mind, 'My wall is loosening' takes on extraordinary resonance. It suggests not simply a process of deterioration, but a loosening of those syntactic, conceptual and verbal controls whereby stark and simple realities — what one might call the radical foreground — are normally distanced, interpreted and subdued. As Auerbach makes clear, the

9.   There was a good deal of this kind of Romanticism in Germany, and it is extensively discussed in Ronald Gray's *The German Tradition in Literature 1871-1945*; see especially Part Two. As an example of this kind of thinking, consider the following remarks by Thomas Mann on the First World War: 'The truth is that all nations together, obeying a higher decree, are labouring for the renewal and rebirth of Europe, of the European soul . . . I believe I can feel . . . something of the Europe that will be afterward: an exhausted Europe, but nevertheless one full of youthful hope, sensitive, purified and appeased by common suffering, reconciled, inclined toward a tender spirituality . . . (*Letters to Paul Amann*, p. 60).

10.   Erich Auerbach, *Mimesis*.

necessary condition of an articulate periodic syntax is a complex world-view in terms of which events can be classified, evaluated and interrelated.[11]

In Yeats's case, such a loosening of syntax and diction may be seen as a deterioration of his rhetoric and philosophy of history; that is to say, he may be breaking down into silence. The important question, however, is whether this impending silence promises isolation and impotence — 'We are closed in' — or whether it convincingly gestures towards something like wise passiveness. Yeats impressively refrains from forcing the issue; but to my mind, even though no attempt is made to specify the conditions for renewal in the body politic, this poem's combination of clarity, honesty and quiet openness suggests the very opposite of paralysis. The loosening wall certainly admits at least the temporary defeat of a way of language; what is more important, it also seems prepared to admit the Minute Particulars of natural kindness.

Note: There are important differences between a thematic and a stylistic approach to this poem. Whereas the former leads one to concentrate upon the problematics of Yeats's bitter-sweet, the latter can skirt these complexities to discover a more significant movement from death to rebirth in the language and syntax. While I think this is an exceptional case (the syntax unusually suggestive, the symbolism unusually suspect), it is a useful reminder that a poem's language can operate in opposition to and in despite of its thematic material.

VII 'I See Phantoms of Hatred . . .'

Vision is certainly the theme of this poem which mentions eyes no less than seven times. From the top of the tower the poet looks out on the countryside, and once again no clear fact can be discerned: 'A mist that is like blown snow is sweeping over all'. Forced back into himself, he looks within for nourishment, and 'Monstrous familiar images swim to the mind's eye'.

His first vision is of maddened soldiers devastating with spiderlike gestures the physical world, just as in 'The Crazed Moon' the fingers of the fly-catchers are 'spread wide that each / May rend what comes in reach':

11.   See particularly Chapters 2-5 of *Mimesis*.

The rage-driven, rage-tormented, and rage-hungry troop,
Trooper belabouring trooper, biting at arm or at face,
Plunges towards nothing, arms and fingers spreading wide
For the embrace of nothing; and I, my wits astray
Because of all that senseless tumult, all but cried
For vengeance on the murderers of Jacques Molay.

(CP 231)

As we saw in '1919', the poet envies the direct expression the soldiers give to a disease which also infects him, and which he can only express in solitary words, strangled cries, and unnatural shrieks of pleasure.[12]

The second vision is of the opposite spiritual condition, the utterly self-possessed being which seeks nothing from its surroundings but bathes in the contemplation of its own fullness. Whereas the spidery troopers manifest the extreme form of lost vision, self-impoverishment and hunger for otherness, the ladies' self-possession is so complete that they have no need to perceive the other, and hence they 'close their musing eyes'.

If the first vision is of Ireland's and Europe's present devastation, the third is a prophecy of what is to come, a vision very similar to the finale of '1919'. Although the troopers are mad, their distraction has a kind of dignity — their eyes have been brightened by the rage for essence and their arms made lean. But when their paroxysm has exhausted itself, Yeats sees not rebirth but numb nightmare following, and an 'indifferent multitude' complacently and without discrimination absorbing whatever is offered to their glazed eyes in a world actually controlled by some totalitarian 'grip of claw' — or so I read it. By furnishing a 'low-definition' image which does not specify exactly the relation between its parts, Yeats provides the reader with a certain interpretative licence. The reading I have suggested does not distort the terms he provides, and is consistent both with '1919' and Yeats's frequent remarks on the tendency of 'democratic' Europe in the twentieth century.

It is interesting to compare this vision, which to my mind is a responsible one, with the hope for the honey-bees in the

12. The envy is expressed directly and calmly in 'The Road to My Door', but there all he admits to envying is the soldier's active life, not his licence to murder.

previous poem, which I find irresponsible. On the one hand, it could be argued that Yeats knew what he was doing, and that to tax him with delusions of alchemical rebirth in 'The Stare's Nest' is to misconstrue an innocuous image. While this is possible, what seems to me more likely is that Yeats, as a chameleon poet, was quite capable of presenting two different versions of twentieth-century collapse in adjacent poems. The question of which one he 'believed' is difficult — indeed for those who hold that the poet never affirmeth it is an illegitimate question. However, this is not the place to go into these matters again, and I would only point out that 'the indifferent multitude' is a more representative Yeatsian utterance than the alchemical honey-bees, and hence I have confined most of my objections to them to a footnote.

In the last stanza we find Yeats reflecting on the detachment which has not only generated the phantoms of this poem but also provided the psychic and physical space in which he could compose the preceding set of meditations. Throughout these poems Yeats's isolation from his society has appeared as a complex fact — both the conscious choice of the banished courtier poet (composing 'emblems of adversity') and the troubled isolation of a man who wants to matter ('To silence the envy in my thought'). His solitude insulates him from the surrounding frenzy so that he can preserve the memory of former civilities, but it also ex-acerbates his estrangement, a condition difficult enough to deal with in normal times. Thus throughout these meditations we find him by turns perplexed by his exclusion ('I complain of the foul weather') and exulting over the fact that amongst the 'innumerable clanging wings' which threaten to besot even his children, he at least is holding out.

In the end Yeats accepts the ambiguity of his position. The abstract joys provide a reasonable compensation for the loneliness they exact and the nihilistic excesses they prompt; and the uneasiness of his situation (neither in the world nor quite free of it, hence the images are only 'half-read') at least keeps him from a quiet old age such as Wordsworth had to endure. [13]   And yet to my mind Yeats is here also considering a rather more significant ambiguity than that of his role of banished courtier who may also be a modern nihilist; and

13.   One similarly senses the contrasting presence of Wordsworth behind the opening section of 'The Tower' (CP 218).

that is, that his poetic isolation may be as much a function of his own personal needs as an heroic response to an evil age.

What makes it possible to see a lowering of the mask in this stanza is the simple directness of the speech. As in 'The Stare's Nest' and 'The Road at My Door' Yeats is here using unrhetorical diction to question the ability of his poetic masks to confront and appropriate the actualities outside his tower. In this final stanza he is questioning not so much his right to the mask of solitary poet as the reasons why he wears it. He resists the rhetoric of high tragedy which would construe him as a great-souled man heroically isolated by a polluted society, a mask he frequently wears with delight. Instead we find the quiet direct language of puzzlement and self-doubt. He wonders if he could have proved his worth in some communal enterprise and then realizes that even had such an enterprise proved completely successful, it would have left him feeling even more insubstantial than he does at present.

This admission sheds significant light on his nostalgia for the good old days at court. The fallen majesty for which he babbles is precisely that, majesty which has fallen, a longing for the past *as past*, not for its return. In this passage he is not only admitting this, but wondering whether this identity may have been thrust upon him not by his noble preference for aristocracy to democracy, and for contemplation to action, but rather by a Faustian disposition which must define itself fantastically in terms of the otherness it negates — in his case, an aristocratic negation of democratic forms and a wordy negation of things.

But 'Faustian' is too rhetorical, too heroic, too mask-like to do justice to the tentative tone of this passage, which to my ear at any rate is considering the possibility that however he may normally construe his life and words as an heroic response to historical drama, its course may have been dictated by a quite personal need to feed the heart on the fantasies of negation. It is a remarkable conclusion to one of Yeats's most remarkable and moving poems.

'Blood and the Moon' (1927)

In this poem Yeats speaks almost throughout as an Irish courtier poet, and explores the nature of his banishment in the tower. The court in question is the Anglo-Irish Ascendancy which presided over Georgian Ireland, and particularly four of its chief spokesmen, Burke, Swift, Berkeley and Goldsmith. Yeats believed that these men and the society from which they came were as civilized as anything Europe had seen since the Renaissance courts of Urbino and Florence, and he frequently referred to the Georgians both in his prose and his Senate speeches as ideals eminently worthy of imitation.

The polar terms which organize this poem and whose opposition it explores are blood and the moon, action and contemplation, power and wisdom, violence and sweetness. Georgian Ireland's greatness is measured by the extent to which it gave unified expression to these two poles of the human spirit, thereby briefly redeeming their tragic disjunction in modern times — a disjunction announced, as we saw, by Hamlet and the spider.

As we might expect, however, this poem is not simply a Georgian elegy. More importantly, it is a Symbolist exercise in self-making, the elaboration of 'my symbol', an attempt to locate in the tower, Yeats's home, the forms of consciousness through which the history of the Irish spirit first 'made articulate and then destroyed the old wild energy'. Just as in the elegy to Robert Gregory Yeats summons to the tower the spirits of dead friends, each one 'a portion of my mind and life', so in this more ambitious poem he ranges through history (mainly Irish but not merely Irish), mastering its significant shapes by fitting them into the tower. Ultimately, by appropriating the essential rhythms of the human spirit, he would become, not unlike Hegel's philosopher of history, all-inclusive and free of the other, identified with the godhead: 'Everything that is not God consumed with intellectual fire.' [14]

In the first section Yeats begins at the beginning, with the Anglo-Normans who built the tower. It arose, he asserts, as a concrete symbol of the Anglo-Normans' power over the Irish, whose old wild energy they ordered and made articulate.

14. 'Now that I am old and live in the past I often think of those ancestors of whom I have some detailed information . . . Then, as my mood deepens, I discover all these men in my single mind, think that I myself have gone through the same vicissitudes, that I am going through them all at this very moment . . . Then I go beyond those minds and my single mind and discover that I have been describing everybody's struggle, and the gyres turn in my thoughts. Vico was the first modern philosopher to discover in his own mind, and in the European past, all human destiny . . . "We can know nothing", he said, "that we have not made". [the spider's motto] . . . so too did Hegel in his *Philosophy of History*' (E 429).

What is remarkable here is that he makes no mention of the Anglo-Normans as an alien power who imposed themselves on a native culture — indeed quite the contrary; they

> Rose out of the race
> Uttering, mastering it.

This distortion of Irish history is significant, though not as significant as Yeats's comparable esteem for the Georgians who effectively dispossessed and banished the old Catholic aristocracy after the Treaty of Limerick (1691). In this poem Yeats is trying to be at home in the tower, and like his predecessors, the Anglo-Normans and the Ascendant Protestants, he ought to face the question of his right to be there, the extremely complex question of his relation to the other in which he would root himself. Failure to do this precludes the possibility of reality and justice obtaining between self and other, and ensures the establishment of estrangement and exploitation.[15]

Perhaps the urgency of Yeats's need to overcome a sense of his social unreality and build a solid selfhood helped to prevent him from facing the problems of guilt and bad faith in the tradition in which he hoped to find himself. In any case just as he does not question the Georgians' right to speak for Irish culture in the second section, so in the first he does not question the legitimacy of the Anglo-Normans, but boldly asserts their organic connection with the land. One finds a comparably confident assertiveness in his famous Divorce Speech in the Senate, where there is no questioning of the Protestant Ascendancy:

15.   Such failure in Yeats's case was certainly not due to ignorance of his ancestral story: 'a Protestant Ascendancy which was to impose upon Catholic Ireland, an oppression copied in all details from that imposed upon the French Protestants' (C 400).

It is also relevant that Yeats helped Frank O'Connor translate 'Kilcash' from the Gaelic. Like 'Blood and the Moon', its subject is the blessing of a house, albeit one which had vanished:

> What shall we do for timber?
> The last of the wood is down.
> Kilcash and the house of its glory
> And the bell of the house are gone,
> The spot where that lady waited
> Who shamed all women for grace
> When earls came sailing to greet her
> And Mass was said in the place.

We against whom you have done this thing are no petty people. We are one of the great stocks of Europe. We are the people of Burke; we are the people of Grattan; we are the people of Swift, the people of Parnell. We have created the most of the modern literature of this country. We have created the best of its political intelligence.

(WBY 371)

Whereas this kind of rhetoric is arguably appropriate to the Senate Chamber, one expects more complex vision to prevail in poetry; as he himself puts it:

> The rhetorician would deceive his neighbours,
> The sentimentalist himself; while art
> Is but a vision of reality.[16]

(CP 182)

To argue that the Anglo-Normans and Georgians were legitimately rooted masters of Ireland would be a difficult task in any circumstances, but is rendered almost impossible in this case by Yeats's choice of emblem; for the first thing that strikes one when looking at any of these towers is precisely their *lack* of connection with their surroundings. Befitting emblems of adversity they may be, but emblems of a power that 'rose out of the race' they most certainly are not. It is surprising that this passage did not precipitate agitation to have him torn for his bad verses.

A profound knowledge of Anglo-Norman and Georgian history is not necessary for one to realize that in both cases the relationship between tower and countryside was not an organic one of father and child, tree trunk and branches, but rather an unnatural one, much more like that of rapist to

---

Here is a fine example of the virtues of parataxis mentioned above (p. 112). When one contrasts this with the adjectival glut that almost paralyses the second section of 'Blood and the Moon', one senses on purely formal grounds that Yeats is having difficulty addressing his subject. According to O'Connor, 'Kilcash' 'was one of Yeats's favourite poems' (*Kings, Lords and Commons*, p. 100).

16. It is worth adding that with his Divorce Speech, the rhetorician only succeeded in needlessly alienating his neighbours. The issue should have been fought as a straightforward case of minority rights. By turning a delicate political issue into an occasion for self-indulgently reminding the mere Irish who the top people were, he ensured failure for his cause (which, clearly, the myth requires).

victim. The tower symbolizes disconnection in the body politic — or rather forced connection — the absence of integrity, not its origin. These towers mocked the land they mastered, and one can be sure, the gesture was returned in kind. Thoor Ballylee's walls did not rise from the battered cottage but were appended to it, a grotesque kind of cubist joke on the past. [17] The final irony here is that since Yeats's domain comprises both tower *and* cottage he must try to be at home in both; hence it is clearly in his interest to assert their unity. But assertion is not enough; tower cannot be joined to cottage until their complex history has been understood, accepted, and forgiven. [18]

Yeats's tower, in short, is a powerful emblem of colonial exploitation, and to this, its most obvious significance, Yeats is blind. The objection is not simply to his distortions of Irish history, but to his failure to recognize the other as other, and its rights to remain other. Insufficiently aware of how the Irish viewed the 'interest' taken in them by the Anglo-Norman and Georgian lords, he is probably analogously uncritical of the interest he has in Ireland.

In the discussion of the spider, we briefly noticed the analogy between the intellectual appropriation of otherness and the colonialists' exploitation of the colonized. In this poem, Yeats is investing himself in a tradition and place which have spidery relations with their surroundings. By not noticing and attempting to dissociate himself from the arachnoid aspect of his inheritance, he confirms it; that is to say, by disguising the spider's parasitic designs on the other, he proves himself one of them, and suggests that far from being driven to seek refuge in the tower by a murderous age, he has, like his ancestors, set himself up in a position of defensive belligerence from which he can launch raids on the inarticulate substance of his countrymen. [19]

17.   'My idea is to keep the contrast between the medieval castle and the peasant's cottage', he said tastefully (L 625).
18.   E.g. The Statute of Kilkenny (1366) forbade miscegenation and it was periodically enforced with considerable savagery. By 1700, however, the 'races' had blended a good deal.
19.   A Marxist critique would go further and attempt to construe Yeats's spidery poetry as an expression of the peculiarly uncertain, parasitic and exploitative position the Anglo-Irish have traditionally occupied in Irish society (both middle-class and Ascendancy — Yeats was the former and aspired to the latter). I am not sure how a Marxist would demonstrate this; luckily my Hegelian prejudices allow me to see not social relations *causing* poetic structure, but rather each illustrating a form of consciousness (*Gestalt des Bewusstsein*) of particular significance for modern man. In any case, their conjunction here produces absorbing poetry.

Having duly noted the presence of the Yeatsian spider, we may return to the poem, whose progress he informs to a remarkable degree. By setting up the tower and the memory of its builders as his home and his emblem, Yeats is verbally re-enacting its original construction. The implication may be that by the sympathetic word-magic of poetry he too is in search of mastery over his surroundings. As paragons of political power and mastery they planted the tree of state which was to reach full bloom in the time of Burke, and their monuments mock the lack of such virtue in the present age. But whereas they mastered the inarticulate with power, blood and stone, Yeats's utterance will be verbal. 'An age is the reversal of an age' and whereas their mastery was real, a bloody ordering of the other's actual substance, his can only be ideal, a verbal ordering of the other's absent substance, its not-self, what it should be and is not. By reproaching his contemporary Ireland with the civil order (*realized* in Georgian times) which it refuses, he might protect himself from its actual disorder and be united with its ideal self whose deathly substance he utters in wise words. Just as his ancestors' power mocks the present lack of it, so he, the last of their line, can only hope for mock-mastery, a verbal semblance of power. And as we have just seen, when he is confronted with the actual presence of contemporary Ireland (in the person of the brown lieutenant) words fail him, and the illusion of mastery is dispelled. I have used the conditional tense to describe the Symbolist solution to the problem of mastery which this poem countenances because though Yeats clearly has it in mind in some sense, he does not actually get down to it in sections three and four, as we shall see.

*

The poem's second section opens with a brief reference to other towers, which prompts some reflection on the tower-symbol as such. Its prime significance for Yeats in this poem is as a symbol of mediation between blood and the moon; with its base firmly anchored in the soil, its top ascends to heaven. The symbolic significance of the towers men build varies a good deal, of course, depending upon whether their prime interests are in looking up or in looking down. The Norman tower, for example, originated as a fairly bloody structure, as Yeats makes clear in the third section. It housed soldiers, and when they climbed the stair it was usually not to contemplate the heavens. Babylonian astronomers on the other hand were fascinated by the heavens but (although Yeats doesn't pause to censure them here) their mathematical approach blinded them to the imaginative mysteries disclosed therein — 'pedantic Babylon' as he says elsewhere.[20] Alexandria's beacon tower illuminated the journeys of those seeking her ancient civilities, and contrasts nicely with Shelley's introspective towers, which Yeats describes in an essay as emblems of the estrangement imposed on the modern prophetic poet (who is 'a man's far-seeing mind' [EI 186]) by a world which does not want to know. Whereas Alexandria's *Pharos* was real, a source of social enlightenment, the towers of such as Shelley and Yeats are ideal, that is, verbal constructs to which banished poets retire, taking as much of the world's substance with them as they can put into words. The light they produce is basically for their own edification — in Shelley's image, songs to cheer their own solitude, not heard, but perhaps overheard.

In the second stanza we are introduced to the Georgians and the tower takes on its most impressive shape: as Yeats puts it elsewhere,

> I . . . suggest . . . that the thought of Swift, enlarged and enriched by Burke, saddled and bitted reality, and that materialism was hamstrung by Berkeley, and ancient wisdom brought back; *that modern Europe has known no men more powerful.* [My italics.]
>
> (E 297-8)

The tower these men inhabit is perfectly poised between blood and the moon, real and ideal; hence Yeats locates them on the winding stair which connects the ground floor with the top. And yet Yeats's treatment of these four is puzzling, for he presents them not as the masters of modern realism which the poem's structure and the above prose passage would lead us to expect, but as four men with a marked preference for moon over blood. Swift for example, of whom Yeats often writes with sensitivity and understanding, makes a crude and excessively noisy entrance beating on his breast because he had the misfortune to be 'dragged . . . down into mankind'.

20.   CP 164. Cf. also CP 240 and CP 8.

This is not a picture of the man who 'made a soul for the gentlemen of this city by hating his neighbour as himself' (M 301), but only of a maddened Platonist having a tantrum — whom Swift admittedly must have resembled on occasion as death and insanity closed him in. Similarly misleading is the description of Goldsmith as an aesthete 'deliberately sipping at the honey-pot of his mind'; locked, as it were, in a narcissistic embrace, clearly having no truck with the world, not even with his own body. This does not square with the Goldsmith Yeats admires elsewhere for his 'delight in the particulars of common life that shocked his contemporaries' (EI 402).[21]

The reference to Burke is also curiously disembodied. All we see of him is his haughty head; which is all that is needed to 'prove' the state a tree if it is only a question of syllogisms, but not enough to compose 'Burke's great melody' (CP 272), that full-bodied song which, as Yeats tirelessly pointed out, was aimed precisely against the bloodless abstractions that lead men to speak vacantly of liberty, equality and fraternity.

Finally, Berkeley and his idealism are misrepresented. Berkeley was no subjective idealist giving every man the licence to think his fantasies substantial; on the contrary, 'all things remain in God' whose mind they express. For Berkeley, this arrangement guaranteed the world's stability and the reality of common meanings, not the reverse — and Yeats knew it: 'Descartes, Locke, and Newton took away the world and gave us its excrement instead. Berkeley restored the world' (E 325). Again, consider the following tribute to the Bishop's organic vision from 'Tom the Lunatic':

'Whatever stands in field or flood,
Bird, beast, fish or man,
Mare or stallion, cock or hen,
Stands in God's unchanging eye
In all the vigour of its blood;
In that faith I live or die.'

(CP 305)

For Berkeley the world is neither preposterous nor a pig, nor does it vanish. Since God's eye is unchanging, these things

21.   Cf. also:
              Oliver Goldsmith sang what he had seen,
              Roads full of beggars, cattle in the fields.   (CP 272)

stand, and rather more substantially than they do in the 'mechanical' philosophies Yeats so despised.

What, one wonders, is going on? Why does Yeats paint such misleading portraits of those four men, portraits whose inaccuracy can be quickly established by referring to Yeats's own writings? What is the relation between these distortions and the mystifications of the Anglo-Norman conquest in the first section? The explanation, it seems to me, is to be sought in what one can infer about the poet's intention.

In this poem Yeats has set out to establish his identity with, or rather his family resemblance to, the Anglo-Normans and the Georgians who travelled his ancestral stair. This involves first of all the assertion of their legitimacy and respectability — hence the problems in section one. Although this question doesn't trouble him nearly as much as it should, he *is* concerned about the legitimacy of his claiming to be of their line. Very simply, they were powerful men and he is not. Their words and actions 'saddled and bitted reality'; his words on the contrary can only aspire to saddle the ideal; to demonstrate, that is, the impossibility of their becoming flesh. As he says in an early poem addressed to his 'old fathers',

> . . . I have nothing but a book,
> Nothing but that to prove your blood and mine.
>
> (CP 113)

In order to prove his blood, he must write this poem which demonstrates the dialectical relationship between blood and the moon, showing that in the present moon-crazed age the pursuit of power is futile and insane, and that a man with mastery in his blood is forced to the top of the tower to seek it in deathly wisdom. Though he lacks the obvious mastery of brute force and loyal servants, he may hope, by fitting all previous masters into his verbal tower, to supervise their immortality and be in effect the masters' master.

What seems likely is that Yeats lost confidence in his ability to prove the dialectical continuity between blood and the moon, that his moon was worthy of (and in a sense contained) their blood. In order to close the gap between him and them, he moves the Georgians upstairs — Berkeley, for example, ends up very close to the top. In short, in the attempt to fit them into his moonlit tower — which is 'emblematical of the night' (CP 266) — he has used his spidery language to make them over into his image. In the third section, however, the Georgians return, and his enterprise is decisively disrupted by the 'Odour of blood on the ancestral stair!'

*

The third section opens with a ghostly paradigm of impregnation:

> The purity of the unclouded moon
> Has flung its arrowy shaft upon the floor.

In contrast to this, the bloody intercourse between the tower's previous occupants and their neighbours is noted with some disparagement. Yeats does not claim kin but leaves them outside, 'there', which is not surprising in view of what we noticed about the first two sections. But suddenly the blood comes inside, mind is invaded by body, present by past: 'Odour of blood on the ancestral stair!' Yeats's attempt to reach the top of the tower is halted by this exclamation mark; and in the following two lines the odour of blood that has reminded him of his own mortality forces him, in effect, to stand on the stair and bay the moon, lunatic. Unable to get free of the ground and those memories that run in the blood, he is caught half-way up the purgatorial stair, having access neither to blood-shedding power nor deathly wisdom. Thus the tower reveals its evil potential, as a prison isolating its occupants from both blood and moon, instead of a place which mediates transactions between the two.

The moon is an ambiguous symbol, for she has traditionally represented both the purity of a timeless simplicity and the complex changes through which humanity moves in response to her waxing and waning: thus she is both virginal and deeply involved with fertility. The Greeks registered this ambiguity in their moon-goddess Artemis by making her both virgin-huntress and the patroness of childbirth.[22] Poets have often found themselves in her service, not only because

22. Aristotle also registers this ambiguity by placing the moon at the boundary between the unmoved heavens and the world they move.

she mediates between the moving and the unmoved, but also because her combination of hunting and chastity aptly symbolizes the potent sterility of poetry. Furthermore, her personal antipathy to childbirth combined with her obligations towards other people's infants is found congenial by celibate poets bearing words which still must help their fellows 'fill the cradles right' (CP 399).

In this poem her chastity is stressed, which again is un-surprising in view of the bloodless tendency of the first two sections; but if one is to make sense of the drunken frenzy in her honour, one must remember that Yeats's moon also has a changing face which bears upon the changing phases of human history, and this, though not brought out by the poet, must be relevant to a poem written 'in mockery of a time half-dead at the top'. At such a time, when the moon is mov-ing into her last phases, she sponsors acts of lunatic violence which bear witness to the general sterility. Thus in '1919' it is she who 'pitches common things about'; and in 'The Crazed Moon', which is placed only four pages after 'Blood and the Moon', she has become 'crazed through much child-bearing', and the poets who traditionally serve her have been turned into 'fly-catchers of the moon', spiders whose fingers are 'spread wide that each may rend what comes in reach'.[23]

These references provide some clue to the lunatic clamour in 'Blood and the Moon'. Either because of the craziness of the time or simply because he is a mortal man, the poet's language lacks the precision which belongs to the arrowy shafts of Artemis the huntress. His words fail to master the blood they pursue, and consequently the displeased goddess requires that he, not unlike Actaeon in the Greek myth, pay for his *hubris* in a drunken orgy of ritual dismemberment. In a waning phase, when the procreative urge produces 'children dazed or dead' (CP 273), the poet must hunt the culture to ground, as the fly-catchers do, and as Yeats has attempted to do in the first two sections. If his verbal arrows miss their mark, then it is he who is 'flung upon the floor', and his own blood must run, to return him to the common condition from which he has tried to rise.

23. In *The King's Threshold*, 'the contagion that afflicts mankind falls from the moon' (CPL 141). In this play, the waning moon sends leprosy to blight the marriage bed, and the celibate poets who serve her are impelled to commit ritual suicide.

In this poem, however, the myth is suppressed. 'We' who must gather on the stair are insipid twentieth-century men, with enough blood to be disturbed by an odour, but not enough reverently to remember the ancient myths and their rigorous logic; and so instead of ritual orgy there is only unconvincing inebriation on the staircase. As in 'Parnell's Funeral' Yeats is either consciously or unconsciously registering the distance that separates present feebleness from ancient sacrifice. The difference is that in this poem he fails even to master his presentation of failure: for section three does not suggest what the relation between blood and moon should be, and the drunken frenzy emerges abruptly from nowhere and disappears as suddenly. Indeed, without extensive knowledge of Yeats's poetry, the reader cannot be expected to put these pieces of language together.

If the gloss I have offered is plausible, the obscure drama in section three is concerned with what happens to poets who reach for the moon. Artemis can both hunt the stag and supervise childbirth without being stained by blood; but she is a goddess, and the poet who would emulate her and forget his own mortality will be reminded of it. In the present age, the failure to escape the blood brings no dismemberment but leaves one in the tower's limbo, neither dead nor alive, only 'half-dead at the top'; for the imperfect poet is only a man, and a man who lacks the stain of blood lacks his proper property. Such virginity looks more like impotence than integrity; for as Crazy Jane the dialectician proclaims,

> . . . nothing can be sole or whole
> That has not been rent.
>
> (CP 295)

Virgins and moon-minded intellectuals may be spared the 'daily pittance' but surely not the 'abstract hatred'; and so with no blood-stain to their credit they are forced through the degrading ceremony on the staircase, to 'clamour in drunken frenzy for the moon'. Because it takes place on a staircase which is neither here nor there, this orgy parodies the truly Dionysiac violence of, for example, the Christian frenzy:

> Odour of blood when Christ was slain
> Made all Platonic tolerance vain
> And vain all Doric discipline.
>
> (CP 240)

Blood tends to be blinding, as Swift's 'sibylline frenzy' indicates, and so too does the drunkenness which runs in the blood: 'A living man is blind and drinks his drop' (CP 266). Stained vision indicates disharmony between self and other, and this condition, which is impressively fought with 'things emblematical of love and war' in the preceding poem, here provokes a much sadder response; for this unconvincingly drunken frenzy promises no regenerative immersion in the 'blind man's ditch' but can only be a barren lament for life lost and wisdom unachieved: it lacks even the lethal dignity which attends the 'fly-catchers of the moon' (CP 273). In the 'natural declension of the soul' (CP 229), the courtier who makes love and war gives way to the spider who makes contact with the mind, and he in turn is undone by the uncertainties infecting the impotent clamour on the ancestral stair. It is a sobering thought, which decisively undercuts the confident enterprise of the opening sections; and if, as I think likely, Yeats had it in mind, it is an admission that substantially redeems the misleading rhetoric from which it is precipitated.[24]

*

The poem's fourth section is subdued and rather uneasy: after such knowledge, what more is there to say? The frenzy is spent, the blood settling, and the moon released from the fierce dialectic. The poem's energy seems slowly to dissipate in rambling speech ('no matter what I said') and an accumulation of images uncertain if they be symbols or 'mere images' ('tortoiseshell butterflies, peacock butterflies'). Largely as a result of this winding down, the gesture at the end towards the moon's inviolable simplicity seems half-hearted,

---

24. Just as I see no way of estimating how conscious Yeats was of his frenzy's implications, so too I cannot estimate the extent to which his 'confession' is made possible by the mannered diction which precedes and envelops it. In ghostly terms, the question is to what extent the odour of blood can be seen as transmitting the Georgians' outrage at their descendant's misuse of language.

unconvinced. One feels that Yeats too has grown tired of the poem, and would like just to *look* at the moon, instead of trying to make something of it.

'The Tower' (1925)

This is one of Yeats's longest and most puzzling poems, whose claims to an over-all unity and coherence are highly questionable. I propose to concentrate on its second section, which on first reading appears to be a series of relaxed interviews with some neighbouring ghosts, loosely organized around a question the poet apparently wants to put to them and yet never quite does. But as is the case with Eliot's Prufrock, one feels that the question is not formulated because it might be overwhelming, and that the poet's composure is continually threatened by the urge to confess some guilty secret.

The question Yeats has in mind concerns the relation between imagination and reality, symbolized here by moon and sun. As in such poems as 'Blood and the Moon' and 'Dialogue of Self and Soul', he is perplexed by their present disjunction, which may be tragic. He is wondering to what extent their opposition is fundamental to the human condition, and to what extent it seems particularly troubling to old men in the twentieth century, such as himself. Thus when he proposes to 'send imagination forth under the day's declining beam' he has at least three questions in mind: under what conditions can imagination prevail in the sunlight? Were conditions more favourable in the past? and above all, is the heart of this old man troubled more by his present exclusion from the dance or by the possibility that his own dealings with sun and moon have been perhaps both dishonest and unworthy of the landscape he has chosen to occupy?

This would be a heavy load of questions for any poem to bear, and it is rendered the heavier in this case by Yeats's oblique approach; irony and analogy keep the poet distanced from anything as crude as straightforward confession. Urbanity is the mask, a formality which both protects him from home truths and makes possible his exposure to them. In short, Yeats has hidden his love away, and 'The Tower' will only yield its secrets to a reader who is willing to undertake patient exegesis; and hence the following discussion will ramble even more than the poem itself.

The first section opens with a cry against old age, followed by an extremely ironic but firm rejection of anything which might resemble 'wise passiveness' as a way of dealing with it. That Yeats is in fact poking fun at Wordsworth here is indicated by 'the humbler worm', which is not at all in the style of the Yeatsian fisherman but a recognizable part of Wordsworth's landscape. The serious point behind this joke is their very different views of the relation between imagination and Nature. Wordsworth believed that the child fathers the man with emotions the adult poet may recollect in tranquillity. Yeats here finds himself in the opposite condition, and is suggesting that despite the absurdities in the posture of 'an old man young' he does not intend to follow 'Wordsworth withering into eighty years, honoured and empty-witted' (M 342). Yeats could probably imagine how Wordsworth found some consolation for his empty-witted old age in the knowledge that 'Nature never did betray the heart that loved her';[25] but since Yeats has spent most of his poetic energies in praise of courtly nonchalance and extravagance, his aesthetic hardly allows for a tranquil senility.

It is important to remember that the courtier poet must merit the company he keeps with an answering 'nonchalance of the hand' (CP 180); like the horsemen he has for companions, he must expose himself to the risks of death, if only at the hands of his mistress; otherwise his poems will grow slack and dishonest. As we have seen, Yeats's enduring problem was to discover forms appropriate to the twentieth century through which he could prove himself a courtier still, not merely a dandy parody thereof; and thus his mockery of Wordsworth here indirectly points to the long quarrel he has had with history and himself about the proper pursuit of human dignity. But even more disturbing than the question of how he is to play out the play is the possibility that a man who really *had* cast a nonchalant eye on life and death should not have survived quite so long. This possibility may indeed be on his mind, for all the ghosts he summons in the second section have had some experience of extravagance and the death that usually claims her servants before their 'natural' span.[26]

---

25. From Wordsworth's 'Lines Composed a Few Miles above Tintern Abbey'.

26. On nonchalance and early death see discussion of 'In Memory of Major Robert Gregory'.

*

The first witness called is a Mrs French who lived near by in the eighteenth century, and though she may qualify as a local exponent of nonchalance, the chief interest of this stanza is in the light it sheds on the Georgian Ascendancy and the manner in which Yeats reflects it. The story of Mrs French is told by her grandson Jonah Barrington in his *Personal Sketches,* which Yeats read in the twenties. As he tells it, the butler mistook the lady's outburst for a veiled request, and the injured party, one Dennis Bodkin, a 'half-mounted gentleman'[27] of the county, chose to pursue the matter at the Galway assizes. As Barrington charmingly puts it, 'They were of course acquitted'; which indicates that in the halcyon days of Georgian Ireland, the half-mounted's sun was no match for the gentry's moon.

To his credit Barrington suggests that Mr Bodkin may not have been altogether to blame for his misfortune: '. . . a sturdy *half-mounted* gentleman . . . who, having an individual mind, entertained an equal aversion to the arrogance of my grandfather and took every possible opportunity of irritating and opposing him.'[28] Thus Barrington almost gives the reader leave to be of Mr Bodkin's party. Such generosity enhances his tale, making it more naughty and yet also more just, indicating that the teller would consider special pleading for the family name somewhat infra dig. Admirers of the genre might even construe it as an example of 'The strength that gives our blood and state magnanimity of its own desire' (CP 269). In any case, within the candidly admitted limitations of his view, Barrington does manage to invest Mr Bodkin with sufficient substance for the reader to suspend his moral judgements in order to enjoy the dramatic play.

Yeats's stanza, on the contrary, makes one uneasy precisely because there is no dramatic conflict. We are not invited to witness an extravagant struggle between French and Bodkin but to admire the whimsical power of silver candlesticks over insolent farmers. Mrs French has a local habitation and a name: the farmer has neither. In effect what we are offered is a cautionary tale, which might be entitled 'Insolence Reproved'. Once one realizes how much inferior Yeats's version is to Barrington's as an example of eighteenth-century

27. An eighteenth-century term for an almost-gentleman, discussed below p. 140.

28. *The Ireland of Sir Jonah Barrington*, ed. Hugh Staples, p.38.

132

nonchalance, one must ask what might have impelled him thus to damage a part of his poem. The short answer is snobbery, but we must read a few more stanzas before we can fully appreciate how it is operating here.[29]

*

Yeats recovers his poise in the next three stanzas, which move from the eighteenth-century manor house to consider how extravagance affected the Catholic peasants some hundred years later. The memory of Mary Hynes, that 'calm and easy woman', has been preserved in local legend by the blind poet Raftery. In an essay Yeats associates her with Helen and Greek tragedy (M 22-30), and the comparison with Maud is taken up at the end of the section.

Writing in 1900 of the legend of Mary Hynes and Raftery Yeats concludes: 'It may be that in a few years Fable, who changes mortalities to immortalities in her cauldron, will have changed Mary Hynes and Raftery to perfect symbols of the sorrow of beauty and of the magnificence and penury of dreams' (M 30). This remarkable sentence illuminates quite accurately the lines he wrote twenty-five years later; for it draws attention not only to the way life can be changed utterly by imagination but also to the ambiguous nature of heroic dreams.

Both Raftery and Mary Hynes died alone and very poor, and Yeats suggests in this early essay that their involvement with the dream of beauty was both cause and effect of their penury. Mary Hynes, having been first taken by a local land-owner as his mistress, was abandoned by him and died young — legend has it that she was 'taken' by the Sidhe, who loved her (M 28). Because of her beauty (in whatever portions real or imagined) she was singled out from the community, first by the 'small local landed proprietor' (A 561), then by Raftery, and then by the gods. Twice Yeats refers to the local belief that 'she had seen too much of the world', and the local sense of tragic Nemesis is nicely summarized thus: 'It is said that no one that has a song made about them will ever

29. Once again, one can indict him with his own words, which makes the charge more significant: 'Even our best histories treat men as function. Why must I think the victorious cause the better? . . . I am satisfied . . . to find but drama. I prefer that the defeated cause should be more vividly described than that which has the advertisement of victory' (E 398).

live long' (M 27). Raftery, for his part, was blind and homeless, and his was the traditional penury and magnificence of the poet who is both divine and outcast; legend has it that only the angels were at his wake (M 30).

This then is the marvellous tale which lies behind these three stanzas in 'The Tower'. Perhaps because at this point in the poem Yeats is not ready to face the question of his relationship with Maud, he does not directly explore the profound implications of Mary Hynes's story, a story which had fascinated him for many years — indeed, 'a peasant girl' is as close as he comes to naming her. To have come any closer might have led him to consider the connections between that 'small local landed proprietor', Raftery, and the gods, and the analogy with his dealings with Maud. He does, however, examine his relations with Maud directly some eight months later in 'Among School Children', and a brief look at its opening stanzas will help the reader appreciate how much his concern with Mary here may be masking.

Like Mary, Maud was singled out from the community by a magnificent dream, a dream of Leda and Helen and high tragedy. As he approvingly contemplates these unheroic school-schildren he wonders how it was that Maud became a 'daughter of the swan'.[30] Some extremely subtle writing in the second stanza suggests that a tale was told of a trivial event that 'changed some childish day to tragedy'; to what extent the day was changed by the event itself and to what extent by the tale is left ambiguous.[31] The repetition of 'told', however, (and its stressed position at the beginning of a line) emphasizes the tale, and also indicates that it was the telling which joined their souls together.

This in turn makes one wonder to what extent Yeats planted the tale in Maud's mind. Both here and in 'A Bronze Head' the implication is that she carried within her from the beginning 'a vision of terror that she must live through', and that this vision had itself 'shattered her soul' (CP 383). But in both poems there is the suggestion that her heroic mask could only appear farcical in the twentieth-century's casual

30. That he did in fact recognize that this is what the children of a new bourgeois Ireland ought to be doing is convincingly argued by Torchiana, IER 123-50.

31. One thinks of the comparable ambiguity in 'Easter 1916', where a childish day is 'changed utterly' to tragedy by an event and the tale Yeats tells of it.

comedy, and the thought of her undoing on both occasions makes the poet 'wild'.[32] In sum, Yeats has two sorts of guilt to consider: first that Maud's song, which he helped compose, was anachronistic and hence unconvincing (which is why the gods did not take her as they took Mary, but let her grow old and 'withered' [CP 382] — like Wordsworth); and secondly, that his poetic interest in her was perhaps an attempt to have her imaginatively instead of engage her humanly. Thus Yeats will have to consider not only that his singing lacks the humility and authority of blind Raftery's, but also that his interest in Maud bears some resemblance to that taken by the 'small local landed proprietor' in Mary.

But in 'The Tower' such considerations will not be registered until Hanrahan is interviewed towards the end. At this point Yeats is concerned only with Mary's song; and so he keeps his distance, playing with the question of moon and sun, and their confusing effect upon the chorus:

> Some few remembered still when I was young
> A peasant girl commended by a song,
> Who'd lived somewhere upon that rocky place,
> And praised the colour of her face,
> And had the greater joy in praising her,
> Remembering that, if walked she there,
> Farmers jostled at the fair
> So great a glory did the song confer.

The stately inversion of 'if walked she there' may strike the reader as unnecessarily formal, even pompous, but in this stanza Yeats is at pains to ask how much of Mary's beauty was the poet's responsibility and yet not provide an answer, which in the circumstances would look like special pleading. To my mind he succeeds admirably, the more so when one considers how important this question was to him, and one anachronistic phrase is a small price to pay for such composure.

---

32. That 'Among School Children' is indeed concerned with trespass is also indicated in this line from the original version:

> And I though never of Ledean kind
> Have wrong to brood upon — enough of that.
>   (V 444)

The first line leads us to expect the realistic testimony of people who actually knew the girl, but what they remember is 'A peasant girl commended by a song'. The long rich sound of 'commended', coming in the middle of the line, effectively joins the peasant girl to the song that envelops her; and the line's satisfying, confident rhythm perhaps suggests that this is how it should be, that any attempt to determine where the girl stops and the song begins would be inappropriate. With the third and fourth lines, however, we seem to be getting information about the girl herself; and the last four seem to be substantiating the view that she really *was* beautiful by enjoyably recalling the fact that farmers *actually* jostled at the fair to catch a glimpse of her. And yet this seeming testimony to her real beauty is questioned by considerable subtlety in the last lines. When they 'praised the colour of her face', the impression is one of direct description of what she was really like. The fifth line, however, indicates that the subject is not simply describing with pleasure the beauties actually inherent in the object, but is also taking some 'greater joy' in the thought that farmers were actually moved to jostle by a song not unlike the one both they and the poet are singing now. Similarly at the end, the picture of the jostling farmers is complicated by the last line. Although they seemed to be simply looking at the object, we discover that in large measure they are responding to the inner lights of their own imaginations which the song has illuminated. The oblique latinate syntax of these lines suspends the jostling farmers between the walking girl and the glorious song, and the reader is left wondering to which of the two the farmers are responding. Again, both the joy and the glory arise in response to the girl's beauty; but equally, both are involved in creating it, and in their self-delighting are not unrelated to the soul singing 'monuments of its own magnificence' in the preceding poem.

Thus Yeats masterfully refrains from judging to what extent her beauty was real, visible in the sunlight, and to what extent it was conferred upon her by the moonlit rhymes which madden the drinkers in the next stanza; and it is just this question which these men determine to resolve. Their expedition is frustrated by 'the great bog of Cloone', but again Yeats refuses to delimit the significance of this incident. Is the man drowned because his *hubris* would not let him live with the marvellous ambiguity of the previous stanza, or is he broken by his refusal to compromise with the dream? The answer must be 'both'.[33]

On the one hand there is his extravagance, his admirable desire to publish his dream, to make it so. But instead of the swan landing on the water, incarnating his desire, a drunkard drowns in a bog. Clearly the time was out of joint; and what has to be considered is the sense in which the revellers' mistake was in declaring it right to 'test their fancy by their sight'. Not unlike Donne's narcissist who sent to know for whom the bell tolls, they assumed that death is what happens to others and that no shadow would fall between their conceptions and reality. The attempt to know the other without taking account of the self's limitations is *hubris*, and drowning in the worldly element is one way of recognizing these.

In a unified age the energies which here produce tragedy or farce would, theoretically at any rate, find real expression in extravagant gestures; for in such an age the moon and sunlight, imagination and reality, can be harmoniously composed. When this is not the case, however, dreams will miscarry, and the gap between imagination and reality opens wide. Failure to recognize this can be seen as either infantile and hubristic or heroically intransigent; or as is usual in tragedy, both.[34] It is because of this 'both' that Yeats has such difficulty in assessing Maud's 'tragedy' and his own. Were they carried away by poetical fantasy or were they maddened by their refusal to give in to an unyielding age? Or were they twentieth-century ironists playing with both possibilities? There can be no simple answer.

*

In the fifth stanza Yeats goes on to consider the 'strangeness' of Raftery's blindness. What may be puzzling him here is not just that a blind man should sing of a girl's beauty, but that he, the part-author of Maud's beauty, is not blind. It is an

33.   Some sense of Yeats's ambiguous feelings towards Celtic dreamers can be found in his early essay on the 'Celtic Element in Literature', where he agrees that the Celtic race may have 'worn itself out in mistaking dreams for reality' but finds this on the whole preferable to the prudence of the English.

34.   In Greek tragedy, the word that best conveys the hero's magnificently mistaken desire to unite the sun and moon is *tolma* or daring, a much more ambiguous word than *hubris*.

important point. In a religious age it is the gods who choose the tragic hero; and whom they would destroy they first make mad. Blind poets, though they may prophesy, do not control the play. Indeed their blindness aptly symbolizes their anomalous position, both privileged and marginal; and daily reminds them that while they may share the gods' wisdom they do not share their power.

The temptation of the Romantic poet in a secular age, as we have frequently noticed, is to mistake his verbal gifts for godly power; and hence when he turns his hand to tragedy he may take the parts of both god and poet. If he does this he will turn into a spider, and his 'tragic' creations will be unconvincing because they are in fact both narcissistic and aggressive. We have seen that spiders are both blind *and* perceptive, and if the tragic prophet can see, one may suspect that he is taking some 'interest' in the sorrow he delivers. [35] To what extent Yeats is considering in this fifth stanza the interest he has taken in his tragic creations is impossible to say; but the last three lines do sound somewhat forced, as if the heavenly afflatus were reluctant to endorse such a windy assertion as 'For if I triumph I must make men mad.' Whether or not one finds the poet uneasy here, he is making it perfectly clear that his tragic enterprise has been a one-man show, and one feels he could hardly be unaware of the risks involved in such 'triumph'.

This feeling is confirmed by the self-mockery in the next two stanzas, which again do not mention Maud but through the figure of Hanrahan definitely bring her closer. He starts off with bold assertion, two more personal pronouns: 'And I myself created Hanrahan'. This assertion and indeed its predecessor, with their heavy pretensions concerning madness and creation, are then nicely undermined by the deadpan conclusion, 'I thought it all out twenty years ago'. The tone of this line makes one think of 'The Circus Animals' Desertion', where, in a much more straightforward way he admits that most of his heroic dramas were actually circus tricks, elaborately propped by 'Lion and woman and the Lord knows what'.

---

35.   Sophocles's Oedipus illustrates the problematic position of the seer when, in an irreverent mood, he doubts Tiresias's disinterestedness *despite* the latter's blindness.

The importance of Hanrahan as a symbol of the poet's evasion becomes clear in the last two stanzas where Yeats finally considers Maud. At this point he is present as one of Yeats's creations, indicating how much times have changed since 'the tragedy began / With Homer that was a blind man'. We have seen that tragic drama must be authorized by the gods if the blind poet is to celebrate the hero's downfall with reverence. But when the gods withdraw the poet stands alone, and his 'tragic' utterance will simply be concerned with inducing various kinds of breakdown. And yet if the drama he creates is ultimately a monologue, the only figures he effectively breaks down are the fantastic projections of his own imagination. Yeats seems to be recognizing his own spideriness in his ironic reference here to the poet's power to 'make men mad', 'drive' them through the dawn, and 'catch' them 'by an old man's juggleries'. [36]

*

The recollections of Hanrahan go on rather too long, as Yeats admits when he terminates them with 'enough!'. With the stanza beginning 'Good fellows' one feels he has strayed so far from the question he promised to ask at the outset that an explicit interruption is called for; and he forces himself — 'I must recall' — to summon a ghost which, unlike the previous ones, has an unconjurable capacity to accuse him.[37]

Brief reflection discloses remarkable similarities between Yeats and this new ghost, similarities which make it obvious

36.   Still, one shouldn't let the irony here allow one to forget the damage such juggling can do. Tragic drama presents human experience in extremity, and the audience is put in touch with its own evil, its profoundest self-contradictions; which is a good thing. The spider poet offers his audience a false version of its own evil: assuming he doesn't do this intentionally, it follows that he thereby puts himself out of touch with his own being, and invites his audience to do likewise. The case of Hanrahan is of course not very significant; but the 'tragedy' Yeats offered Maud and himself, and indeed Ireland, is more serious: for example, 'Did that play of mine send out certain men the English shot?' (CP 393).

37.   The similarities I find between Yeats and this man go considerably beyond the connections Yeats explicitly makes in this poem. Some justification for this lies in the poem's complexity; and Yeats's commitments to the mask guarantee that any confessional poetry he writes will be oblique. Nevertheless my reading does involve reading *in*, and on lines very close to the ideas developed in the discussion of 'Blood and the Moon'.

why Yeats has had to *force* himself to recall this man. Both are not quite landed gentlemen of negligible means, uncertain of their tenancy, and both are immobilized by the sun's glare of which they have not taken sufficient account. Though in different ways, each has played with extravagance but lacked the substance to make it actual. The wasteful virtues can only earn the sun if there is something there to waste. One thinks of an early poem:

> How should the world be luckier if this house,
> Where passion and precision have been one
> Time out of mind, became too ruinous
> To breed the lidless eye that loves the sun?
>
> (CP 106)

The house is ruined when it no longer breeds the eagle's lidless eyes that love the sun; that is, eyes which enable it to swoop with precision upon the object of its desire. In 'The Tower' similarly, both ancient and present master of 'this house' have lost the ability to move upon their moonlit energies, and hence become dogs staked out in the yard — the one bound by financial debts, the other by old age and an environment he cannot master, which includes the debts of a lifetime spent, mis-spent, and unspent.

The bankrupt master represents the ruination of a tradition of military men to whom the neighbourhood was in several senses 'indebted'; and as 'an age is the reversal of an age', so threatening did this neighbourhood become that some say the ancient master could leave the tower only on Sundays, others that he 'hid in the secret passage'.[38] We have considered Yeats's inability to cope with his environment and his ancestors at some length in the discussions of 'Blood and the Moon' and 'Meditations in Time of Civil War':

> We are closed in, and the key is turned
> On our uncertainty.
>
> (CP 230)

In this poem he does not specify whether it is his or the bankrupt's sleep which is haunted by the memory of their heroic fathers, but surely it is both.

---

38. Yeats's notes to the poem (CP 532).

Perhaps the most important aspect of the bankrupt master is that he was a man who, though perhaps extravagant in some sense (that is, some former time) was unable to make contact with the neighbourhood because he could not pay. In other words he was a fraud, who attempted to seem more substantial than he was. Yeats's extravagance has also been somewhat fraudulent, a mastery of words not things; and his failure to ground himself either in the tower or modern Ireland is aptly summarized in his non-engagement with Maud, which closes the section. But before we leave the bankrupt we must briefly consider the question of class.

Yeats, the bankrupt, 'the small local landed proprietor', and the insolent farmer, all look suspiciously like 'half-mounted gentlemen'; that is, middle class, almost certainly Protestant, with a tenuous hold on the land, eager to disassociate themselves from those in trade, and yet clearly aware that Mrs French can have their ears docked if they get bumptious. [39]   It must have been a disquieting position to occupy on the social ladder. As the image of being 'half-mounted' suggests, it was neither here nor there, an exposed and ungainly position from which it was difficult to rise, easy to fall. Indeed, in many ways it was rather a non-position — neither gentry, nor professional, nor commercial, nor Catholic, nor peasant, but frequently mocked and suspected by each of these.[40]

39.   Indeed Yeats provokes this association by referring to the bankrupt as a 'half-mounted man', which was Barrington's term for the insolent farmer.

40.   As Yeats said: 'We were merchant people of the town. No matter how many thousands a year our mills or our ships brought in, we could never be county, nor indeed had we any desire to be so . . . the long settled habit of Irish life had set up a wall' (cited in Torchiana pp. 185-6). To be exact, Yeats was rather less than half-mounted. On his mother's side the Pollexfens were merchants, whereas the Yeatses left off trading in the eighteenth century, and acquired some land and professional status. Yeats's grandfather and great-grandfather were both clergymen. Yeats's father — from his letters a most attractive gentleman — was a portrait painter, whose canvases brought in very little money, which perplexed his in-laws. W. B. lacked his father's refinement and generosity, but perhaps such qualities are incompatible with genius. In the above passage when Yeats says 'We were merchant people', this is true enough for so they were regarded. But also it serves his dramatic purpose which in this case is to emphasize the gap between Yeats and Gore-Booth, a gap which he set out to bridge in poetry. The important point here is that he thought of this bridging as restoring the family name to its original dignity, not as a thrusting attack upon the citadel. (Cf. George Moore in *Vale*: 'Yeats . . . had said that if he had his rights he would be Duke of Ormonde'.) In short his position was that much more painful than the half-mounteds'; for he lacked their visible substance ('Yeats, we both belong to the lower middle classes', ibid., p. 16) and yet was more convinced than they of his right to be king.

Although generalizations about class characteristics are notoriously dangerous, one can at least suggest that to be half-mounted in Ireland, from the eighteenth century to the early twentieth century, was to be exposed and vulnerable, and hence tempted to adopt a posture of 'defensive bellige-rence'[41] towards one's surroundings. Yeats's treatment of the insolent farmer in the earlier stanza is certainly belligerent, and also to my mind, defensive. Indeed, it is an arresting instance of class-swapping, with suggestive self-destructive implications. One recalls George Moore:

> It is impossible to imagine the hatred which came into his voice when he spoke the words 'the middle classes'; one would have thought that he was speaking against a personal foe; . . . and we asked ourselves why Willie Yeats should feel himself called upon to denounce the class to which he himself belonged essentially, on one side excellent mer-cantile millers and ship-owners, and on the other a portrait painter of rare talent . . .
>
> (*Vale* pp. 160-1)

By the tenth stanza of the second section, however, when Yeats says 'Come old, necessitous, half-mounted man', he has implicitly accepted his connections with the middle classes — in a sense, accepted Moore's reprimand; and how much it cost him to do so is perhaps betrayed by the hysterical wit of 'Gifted with so fine an ear'.

*

In the tenth and eleventh stanzas it seems as if Yeats is inter-rupting his narrative to summon all the ghosts together in order dramatically to put his question to them. But the question is badly phrased, it's not quite what the poem has been about (despite its introduction in section one); and the ghosts (plus the reader), realizing that Yeats is not yet ready to confess and present himself for judgement, admonish the poet with 'eyes that are impatient to be gone'. He in his turn accepts the justice of this and releases us with 'Go therefore'; but Hanrahan is to stay behind, for being so like Yeats himself

---

41. This is the expression I used in the discussion of 'Blood and the Moon' to describe Yeats's spidery activities in the tower.

he is less threatening, and will perhaps sympathetically receive Yeats's final secret, his overwhelming question:

> Does the imagination dwell the most
> Upon a woman won or woman lost?

It is important to notice that the only ghost in this company Yeats can reveal himself to is one who never actually lived in the neighbourhood but only in Yeats's imagination; which aptly illustrates how much Yeats is 'closed in'. And yet even here he does not mention Maud but asks Hanrahan to admit that *he* turned aside from *his* lover. In short, by thus 'confessing' to one of his own puppets he maintains to the end his determination to make an inventory of his sins without actually naming one of them! This he can do because, unsurprisingly, Hanrahan's secret is very like Yeats's own. Though he may be remembered as an old lecher with mighty memories and a reputation for fine poetry, we already know he was more circus animal than hero. What hasn't been mentioned yet is that he was a poet who neglected human love for the muses who in turn rejected him as 'weak' and 'afraid', unworthy of their company. At the end of the story referred to in stanzas six and seven, he is left, like many figures in Yeats's early verse, neither drunk nor sober, fully engaged neither by the muses nor human society (M 213-24). That Yeats doesn't remind him of this until they are alone is another fine irony in this most ironic poem.

*

The poem's final section is marred by ill-tempered rant, and signally fails to resolve or even acknowledge the profound and moving testimony which precedes it. Yeats is writing his will:

> I choose upstanding men
> That climb the streams until
> The fountain leap, and at dawn
> Drop their cast at the side
> Of dripping stone; I declare
> They shall inherit my pride.

This makes a pretty picture but it is an image from his younger days (CP 166) with little relevance to the present question of whether Yeats is the last of his line. Such men, for all that rather laboured sexual imagery, could never manage Hanrahan's mighty memories; nor are they substantially connected to the landscape. Indeed, the more one looks at them the more they look like a poster from the Irish Tourist Board; and if one asked their names, they would probably turn out to be English visitors.

Whether or not they are English, the poem at least makes it clear that they must be Protestant. But the problem is not just religious: what this poem requires is men who will carry on the attempt to implant in Ireland the (not exclusively Protestant) values and memories Yeats has tried to serve; and for this task something heavier than elegant movements through the dawn is required. In the lines which follow, Yeats seems to sense that his cast has failed; for the image of the fisherman turns into that of the dying swan, his favourite emblem for the solitary and vanishing poet.

But the question of inheritance is not ultimately decisive, for even without progeny Yeats can still hope that death may be met with composure:

> I have prepared my peace
> With learned Italian things
> And the proud stones of Greece.

The contemplation of such abstract things will gradually cause the Irish ground to fade away, and in the last passage he closes the door on his Irish landscape, the memories this poem has illuminated. If he has brought both reality and justice to his interview with the tower's ghosts, he may hope they will depart and trouble him no more. In a sense this poem has reversed the process begun in the Robert Gregory elegy, in which the poet moving into the tower was attempting to invite a number of personal ghosts to supper. In this poem, written in the shadow of a serious illness, Yeats's uncertainty as to whether death is near is aptly figured in his uncertainty as to whether the ghosts want to leave him and whether he wants them to go away. In any event the door closes, and he hopes henceforth so to fix his attention on Byzantium's unchanging light that he may not mind his own sun setting; and the poem ends with a premonition of this, one of the most attractive deaths in English poetry.

DEATH MASKS

Greater glory in the sun,
An evening chill upon the air,
Bid imagination run
Much on the Great Questioner;
What He can question, what if questioned I
Can with a fitting confidence reply.

(CP 278)

Clowns who live to please must please to live; and in a tragic age the fool whose true master is either dead or absent must not only sing for his supper but also satisfy the ghost of his absent Lord. Thus his song will be a mixture of present laughter and the gravity of ancestral voices, and this gravity will be both a judgement on the present and a submission to the past. But since the past masters to whom he would submit and from whom he would receive authority to reject the present are more or less dependent for their presence on his imagination, the fool may come to wonder if he is not serving only the creatures of his own fantasy. We shall see Yeats examining his clownish career in 'High Talk' and 'The Circus Animals' Desertion'.

A remarkable amount of his later poetry is troubled by the prospect of judgement; such themes as pride, humility, vindication, forgiveness, remorse and absolution recur frequently, and Yeats's difficulty in getting the answers right is less surprising when one remembers that the ground from which he drew the justification for his denunciations of present evil was located mainly in his imagination of an aristocracy that was and is no more. This had been so even in 1914:

While I, from that reed-throated whisperer
Who comes at need, although not now as once
A clear articulation in the air,
But inwardly, surmise companions
Beyond the fling of the dull ass's hoof
— Ben Jonson's phrase — and find when June is come
At Kyle-na-no under that ancient roof
A sterner conscience and a friendlier home . . .

(CP 143)

But if in his poetry he effectively masters the ghosts he seems to serve, then there is some question of their competence to preside over his soul in judgement: and as we have seen, Yeats was aware that such imagined (and perhaps imaginary) ground may not provide sufficient support for a man whose aspirations to verbal authority require that he be able to kneel if he is finally to stand. But if his ground is not in Coole Park, where might it be?

One of the clearest expositions of this dilemma is 'The Municipal Gallery Revisited' (1937), in which the poet is looking for an answer in the images of Ireland's past thirty years. Each stanza presents us with pictures of Irish pride, humility and reverence, and Yeats is wondering in this public place if there is not some further common ground, some spiritual municipality in which all these gestures of noble authority and extravagance are rooted. If there is and if he has served it too, then his gestures may be judged as substantial as theirs, to whom he is united by a reverence which transcends and perhaps to some extent redeems the hatreds which have consumed his country and embittered his life.

The first two stanzas suggest an impressive and uncharacteristic catholicity. What is significant about the revolutionary soldier and the Archbishop is not their political postures but the fact that like Augusta Gregory, both their pride and their humility may be located in the common ground of reverence, the ultimate source of significance. And yet for whatever reasons, Yeats cannot sustain the generous faith necessary to engage the complexities of modern Irish history and still manage to see all these figures folded in a single party. Perhaps as he contemplates the destruction of Coole in the fourth and fifth stanzas it occurs to him that politics and warfare have effectively uprooted and destroyed the ground of Irish reverence, and hence at least some of the figures in the first two stanzas must have been worshipping in a very different church; in which case to kneel with the enemy would be sacrilege. In any event the remaining five stanzas concentrate increasingly on the virtuous Anglo-Irish, so that one is not surprised when Yeats asserts rather aggressively of Lady Gregory, Synge and himself;

We three alone in modern times had brought
Everything down to that sole test again,
Dream of the noble and the beggar-man.

In short, Yeats fails to ground himself in the soil of modern Ireland; and as if in scorn of such an enterprise he registers the triumphant defeat of the Anglo-Irish in 'an image out of Spenser and the common tongue'. The ground on which he and his friends kneeled may now be fouled by the modern fox but it none the less persists undefiled in the ideal spaces of his poetry; and thus a poem which began in the search for common prayer ends in the proud defiance of its impossibility. We have come a long way from 'Easter 1916'.

This poem, though magisterial in some respects, leaves us uneasy on several points. To what extent, for example, does Yeats realize that he has written a very unbending poem about his desire to kneel? Does he intend to deny the ground of revolutionary soldier and Archbishop as he affirms the 'dream of the noble and the beggar-man'? How solid is the ground of that dream in the twentieth century? How legitimately may he claim kin with Synge, or for that matter with Lady Gregory? How strong can a man grow from contact with ideal soil, soil which is at best a sacred memory and at worst a projection of his own fantasies? Is not the primary feature of soil from which the dialectic of pride and humility may rise that it be *other* than the self which would be grounded in it? Finally, has he bent his knees to anything more substantial than his own ideal conception of himself and his friends? Such questions as these will inform this chapter's discussion of some of Yeats's last works.

'Parnell's Funeral' (1933)

In this poem Yeats turns again to one of his deepest concerns, the perverted return of Dionysiac energies on to a stage where few if any of the players can remember much of what this ancient god actually commends. By measuring the distance between ancient sacrifice and its parody in contemporary Ireland, Yeats provides both a devastating indictment of twentieth-century feebleness and an opportunity to estimate his own implication in it.

The second stanza stamps out the sacrificial rhythm with typical Yeatsian gravity: and although we have already discussed several aspects of this tragic story, its importance and complexity can easily bear some further commentary.[1] In the ancient Mediterranean the Great Mother was variously known

1. See Jeffares's *Commentary* for background material.

as Cybele, Aphrodite or Demeter, and the boy (usually her lover or her son) as Attis, Adonis or Dionysus.[2] As vegetation goddess she required the boy's dismembered body every year in ritual recognition of the seasonal cycle. In Greek myth Dionysus was liberated from strictly seasonal obligations and came to represent certain violent energies which were celebrated through the ritual tearing and eating of his flesh. In the Christian myth similarly, the ritual ingestion of the dismembered Christ is a consecration of divinely disreputable energies. It was Yeats's view (which he may have found in Frazer's *Golden Bough* [3]) that the worship of Dionysus and Christ (and other Near-Eastern deities) was subversive of the Apollonian orders in classical civilization; and he explores the similarities between these two gods in his play *The Resurrection*, from which two songs appear in the *Collected Poems*:

The Roman Empire stood appalled:
It dropped the reins of peace and war
When that fierce virgin and her Star
Out of the fabulous darkness called.

(CP 240)

When Gods such as Dionysus and Christ are torn and eaten, the energies they embody are both renounced by *and* transmitted to the congregation. In crude terms, the 'pierced boy' represents the innocent and anarchic energies upon the renunciation or sublimation of which civil society is at least partially constructed; and the 'Great Mother' represents that civil order which is both appalled by the manifestation of these energies and yet nourished by their sacrifice. Thus the play which ritually enacts God's death both acknowledges the criminality of society as such and to some extent redeems it. The paradox here is that a society's bonds are strengthened through the ritual incorporation of the energies it cannot tolerate: as Auden puts it,

For without a cement of blood (it must be human, it must be innocent) no secular wall will safely stand.[4]

('Vespers', *The Shield of Achilles*)

2. The currency of this myth in the Mediterranean is indicated in the poem (rather confusingly) by the 'Cretan barb' being stamped on a 'Sicilian coin'.
3. See Chapter 37.
4. On the general nature and function of human sacrifice, see Hubert and Mauss, *Sacrifice*, especially Chapter 5. See also Frazer's *Golden Bough*.

For William Blake, from whom Yeats received a good deal
of his mythic education, the Great Mother is the Woman Old,
embodying the vegetable glass of Nature, an oppressive social
order, and indeed everything which conspires against Imagina-
tion:

> And if the Babe is born a Boy
> He's given to a Woman Old,
> Who nails him down upon a rock,
> Catches his shrieks in cups of gold.

(B 111)

Blake did not hesitate to call the boy Christ; and by this he
simply meant the imaginative vision of organized innocence
which society, both through its institutions and its individuals,
always puts down.

Blake was by no means the first poet to find himself in the
mythic struggle between woman and boy. At least since the
time of Orpheus artists have suspected that this story bears
upon their activity; and Yeats was no exception, as we have
frequently noticed.[5] Thus when we read 'Parnell's Funeral',
we must recognize that like so many of Yeats's most
important poems ostensibly about someone else, it also
provides a fine opportunity for self-dramatization.

*

> Under the Great Comedian's tomb the crowd.
> A bundle of tempestuous cloud is blown
> About the sky; . . .

From this deadpan suggestion of a fragmented and secular
congregation, in which the crowd is hardly distinguishable
from the cloud, Yeats moves quickly to wonder whether this
occasion has any connection with primitive ritual. A redeemer
has been murdered by his people: hence it is not inappro-
priate to look for 'the holy hush of ancient sacrifice'[6] — all
the more so because of the shooting star seen by many of the
mourners at the funeral.[7]

5. Robert Graves goes further: 'All true poetry . . . celebrates some incident or
    scene in this very ancient story' (*White Goddess*, p. 24).

6. Wallace Stevens, 'Sunday Morning'.

7. See Yeats's commentary on the poem in *Variorum*, p. 832 ff.

But instead of Holy Communion Yeats finds its parody. The cloudy crowd obscures the real significance of 'a star laid low'; and as the poem's second section makes clear, the 'shudders' that run 'through all that animal blood' have more to do with titillation than profound convulsion. Not unlike the shrieking weasels of '1919', these animals are thrilled by a devastation they caused but will not authorize. For them it is no tragic sacrifice, but something farcically played 'Under the Great Comedian's tomb', which like the alien murders of Emmet, Fitzgerald and Tone, 'had not touched our lives'. If the blood is not drunk and the guilt not accepted, then instead of a redemptive sacrifice all we find is voyeurism, surely the most characteristic perversion of our time.

When Yeats says 'None shared *our* guilt' he is admitting his implication in the farcical drama of recent Irish history. Though he played no part in the scandal-mongering that dragged Parnell down, he did have a significant role in the general failure to build a stage on Irish ground upon which dramatic life could appear. The 'painted stage' brings to mind 'The Circus Animals' Desertion', where he admits that his lifelong concern with 'Players and painted stage' evaded rather than engaged the heart-mysteries that run in the blood. [8] Ireland's failure to engage these mysteries is strikingly symbolized on the occasion of Parnell's funeral; and Yeats is wondering if such failure may be mitigated through poetic testimony; that is to say, whether some ideal common ground may be constituted in a Symbolist poem which grants its real impossibility.

But in the silence that separates the third and fourth stanzas the poet is overcome by the almost ludicrous implausibility of his tentative gestures towards common prayer. This is no congregation, only a crowd of mean-minded and hypocritical voyeurs, many of whom are Roman Catholic. Hence he rises from his knees, disowns the 'we' of the third stanza, and defies the throng. For the rest of the poem, much as in 'The Municipal Gallery Revisited', he attempts to dissociate himself from the mere Irish and proclaim the un-dismayed fellowship of Swift, Parnell and Yeats, the masters of Anglo-Irish solitude.

8. Cf. also the discussion of '1919', and 'Blood and the Moon'. Also, in the light of this discussion, one can read the line 'Did that play of mine send out certain men the English shot?' as a confession not of heroic guilt but of fatal frivolous-ness.

But how can it be done? The fourth stanza is extremely perplexing: on first reading it seems as if Yeats is asking to share Parnell's fate and be torn for his bad verses. This idea is in itself almost indigestibly hyperbolic. But on reflection one sees that it cannot even be this 'simple': for how could Yeats's thirst for accusation be satisfied by a throng which holds no brief for the kind of 'human liberty' he has tried to serve? [9] Thus at some unconscious level the accusing eye Yeats has in mind must be Parnell's, whose ghost he is imploring to come and hear how Yeats has not altogether sustained the Anglo-Irish tradition of solitary integrity; for only Parnell's ghost would be wise enough to know in what sense the noise Yeats made as a sometime nationalist and trainer of circus animals was blarney, masking the death-rattle of Irish culture. [10] On the other hand Parnell's ghost is no Great Mother; only the Catholic Paudeen has the power to rend, and confer upon Yeats the sanctified rejection which graces Parnell. Therefore, if this reading is legitimate, the scene we must envisage is Parnell's ghost as priestly confessor, and the throng as executioner.

But can *this* be done? Is such a scene rich in ambiguity or is it absurdly self-contradictory? I suggest it is the latter, and that the contradiction involved is a profoundly significant one, identifying a Yeatsian dilemma which cannot be resolved even in the ideal terms of this poem.

Yeats would submit himself to judgement: but to submit to Paudeen is inconceivable. Only the departed ghosts of Anglo-Ireland could make a fitting tribunal — which means that they were the only ones he was talking to and for all along. Consequently he cannot expect Paudeen to be interested in tearing him as she tore Parnell: and if his body is refused by the Great Mother, it may be bloodless, it may be nowhere; in which case he may not qualify for admission to Jonathan Swift's dark grove. [11]

9. Cf. CP 277.

10. Support for identifying 'the accusing eye' as Parnell's can be found in other poems where Yeats would submit to the judgement of Anglo-Irish ghosts: for example, 'In Memory of Major Robert Gregory', 'Demon and Beast', 'Blood and the Moon', 'In Memory of Eva Gore Booth', 'The Tower', 'The Municipal Gallery Revisited'.

11. One thinks of the bloodless frenzy in 'Blood and the Moon' where Yeats is comparably disturbed by Swift's ghost.

Such is the real horror underlying the poem, perhaps only partially glimpsed by the poet. However, in a commentary upon 'Parnell's Funeral' Yeats does make a statement which fits this discussion very well: 'George Bernard Shaw, Oscar Wilde, George Moore, the most complete individualists in the history of literature, abstract, isolated minds, without a memory or a landscape' (C 401). This is a consummate description of the Anglo-Irish dilemma in the late nineteenth century: and it is Yeats's dilemma. Memory he most certainly has; landscape, as this book has tried to show, is by no means certain. This leaves individualism; and the fourth stanza of this poem is part of the evidence.

What remains to be said about 'Parnell's Funeral', however one construes its fourth stanza, is that even if Yeats does qualify for an end like Parnell's — that is, even if he *has* offered himself to Ireland — it would be sheer fantasy to suppose that he might nourish with his 'death' an Ireland he could not nourish with his 'life'. If Parnell was indigestible Yeats would be all the more so; for the bitter wisdom plucked in this dark poem is that the Great Mother has lost her sacred bow. Although she still kills, she does so absent-mindedly, and the heart is no longer cut out. Yeats knows that in some sense Great Mother Ireland has refused him her ground: but in *what* sense and *why*? Though I have suggested some answer, the poem provides none, and hence it leaves Yeats in limbo, his thirst for accusation and judgement unslaked.

The failed communion of Parnell's funeral does compose a powerful image for the dramatic failure of modern Ireland. The refusal to devour Parnell's heart means that the murder is left unnamed, unconfessed and unredeemed, the crowd unsanctified and estranged from its own blood, each member languishing absently in some parody of ghostly solitude. As a member of this crowd Yeats languishes too: as the last of the Anglo-Irish masters he can seek in Parnell's actual death a metaphor of his own ill-defined lack of social connection; and as the author of this Symbolist poem, he can present those absent energies by which alone these present obliquities may be judged.

'High Talk' (1938) and 'The Circus Animals' Desertion' (1938)

The priests of all ages have always pretended that they wished to 'improve' . . . But we of another persuasion would laugh if a lion-tamer ever wished to speak to us of his 'improved' animals. As a rule, the taming of a beast is only achieved by deteriorating it.[12]

This passage is typical of Nietzsche in a restless mood, impatient of the late nineteenth-century's thin-blooded comedy, and rather looking forward to the return of wild animals in twentieth-century cataclysm. When a culture becomes over-refined, it takes for an improvement of Nature what is in fact a degradation of it. Thus for example, when cavalry officers would rather laugh at circus lions jumping through hoops than train their horses to carry them through danger, decadence has arrived: 'When a civilization ends, task having led to task until everybody was bored, the whole turns bottom upwards, Nietzsche's "transvaluation of all values" ' (E 433).

Like Nietzsche Yeats knew he lived in decadent times and that for all his efforts, his poetry must be decadent too. This can be readily observed in the golden birds of the Byzantium poems. As representations of the alchemy whereby art can complete and perfect nature by purging it of its bloodiness they may be thought supremely civilized; but like the golden grasshoppers in '1919' they also look like the playthings of a decadent culture, serving only 'to keep a drowsy Emperor awake' (CP 218).

The circus, viewed as comic drama, is a parody of culture. Instead of the alchemist finding life in its absence we see the conjuror producing rabbits from hats; and though the lion-tamer in his cavalry breeches may produce a *frisson* with his whip, the real master of ceremonies is the clown, suggesting in his dropsical floppiness that whatever the culture may once have mastered 'has run wild', as Yeats's Malachi puts it. We cheer when the clown mocks the lion-tamer, we worry when he gets caught in the lion's cage, and we are dismayed when his tears tell us that all is by no means well.[13]

'High Talk' (1938)

Malachi was the last of the Old Testament prophets, and his namesake in the twentieth century may be one of the last of

12.   Nietzsche, *The Will to Power*, section 397.

13.   In Yeats's time the circus was still in business, but as we move further into the century the performers go mad and begin to appear in people's nightmares. Hence Pozzo the lion-tamer and Lucky the clown in Beckett's *Waiting for Godot*.

the prophetic clowns. The stilts he walks on are the metaphors through which European poetry has attempted to amplify and dignify human experience. His great grandad's were twenty feet high; and though his are only fifteen, 'no modern stalks upon higher'.

The serious point behind this burlesque is that poetic metaphor once *did* amplify human experience. When man believed himself half-devil, half-angel, he was appearing on a larger stage than he does now: both sin and sublimity were within his reach. In Yeats's view, as we have seen, the comedy set in with Shakespeare, and by the time of Malachi's great grandad the metaphors were discernible as such: that is, stilts which make man seem larger than he is, stalk in ungainly fashion, and lose connection with the earth that bears him. Because of this, some sensible rogue saw that Malachi's stilts were a waste of good timber and 'stole them to patch up a fence or a fire'. We have come a long way from the burning of that sacred 'stump on the acropolis' in '1919'.

Like the good clown that he is, Malachi seems to have enjoyed the joke. But the show must go on, and so he 'takes to chisel and plane' for a new pair, which he constructs in the final section.

Here the tone changes as Malachi declares that 'whatever I learned has run wild'. Instead of returning to console the circus-goers, he decides to follow the honest rogue's example and admit the show is over. So he builds a pair of apocalyptic stilts and stalks off into the night to find the wildness. There he meets the barnacle goose, whose 'wind-blown clamour' was heard by a mad beggar many years before, announcing the end (CP 128).[14] When 'night splits and the dawn breaks loose' Malachi is terrified but stalks on; for his new stilts have put him in touch with Great Nature, and if he is brave enough he may join at the end in 'God's laughter at the shattering of the world' (CPL 114).

It is an astounding poem, which masters the nihilism that nearly undermines the earlier and similarly apocalyptic '1919'. In the intervening twenty years Yeats had learned how to move on short stilts; had learned, that is, how to dismantle the complex rhetoric of high culture, with its abstruse and mystifying metaphors from history, and to speak on certain occasions like the mad Irish fool who had haunted him for so long. The stage is almost set for Samuel Beckett to come on.

14. Cf. the swan in '1919', riding 'those winds that clamour of approaching night'.

154

'The Circus Animals' Desertion' (1938)

This poem, though similar in theme, bears no trace of the extraordinary energy which pervades 'High Talk'. Yeats is thoroughly dejected, and even the magnificent Malachi looks like one of 'those stilted boys'. On this occasion Yeats is seeking the man behind the masks; and instead of stalking on into the embrace of cultural death he is proposing to abandon metaphor altogether, and simply die. But 'proposing' is the key word here: this critique of metaphor is conducted through metaphor, and the 'naked' man at the end is still well masked. Though by no means a dishonest poem, its language is so abstract that the real issues are not properly engaged, and this precipitates an uncharacteristic error of judgement in the final section.

The bulk of the poem reviews his early work in praise of heroism and courtliness, and what strikes him about it now is its anachronism. These tales were fit to 'adorn old songs or courtly shows' but not to revive Irish life. Although invocation of the past is a traditional way of dramatizing the present, escape to the past is a traditional way of avoiding the present; and in Yeats's case it was not just the cultural emptiness of the twentieth century but also the thwarted love affair with a lady called Maud. Regarding the former, there is an illuminating passage in one of Yeats's journals:

> I have felt when re-writing early poems . . . that by assuming a self of past years, as remote from that of today as some dramatic creation, I touched a stronger passion, a greater confidence than I possess, or ever did possess. Ezra when he re-creates Propertius or some Chinese poet escapes his scepticism . . . I feel as neither Eliot nor Ezra do the need of old forms, old situations that, as when I re-create some early poem of my own, I may escape from scepticism. [15]

As with Eliot and Pound, scepticism was Yeats's enduring problem, and now that the show is over he is willing, almost eager, to admit it.

Thus a sceptical and embittered heart was the secret which the magic in 'those masterful images' had attempted to conceal. The ring-master in his fancy gear may have seemed to be moving his animals in a lively way, suggesting that body was

15.   Unpublished journal quoted in Ellmann, *The Identity of Yeats*, p. 239.

still harnessed to mind, but in fact Malachi was right, the old learning had 'run wild'. When the heart is embittered and exhausted, the only sorts of images that can sustain the illusion of mastery are those that 'grow in pure mind'.

In the final section the secret heart is opened and we are invited to inspect its contents:

> A mound of refuse or the sweepings of a street,
> Old kettles, old bottles, and a broken can,
> Old iron, old bones, old rags, that raving slut
> Who keeps the till.

Here Yeats's dejection has undermined his judgement, for this is unconvincing hyperbole. From such a junkyard very few ladders could start, certainly not 'all' of them, nor indeed the ones on which the Yeatsian troupe has clambered for so many years. Although this passage badly damages the poem, we can perhaps retrieve our discussion of it by considering an outstanding piece of prose upon which these lines may have been based:

> Tolstoy in *War and Peace* had still preference, could argue about this thing or that other, had a belief in Providence and a disbelief in Napoleon, but Flaubert in his *St. Anthony* had neither belief nor preference, and so it is that, even before the general surrender of the will, there came synthesis for its own sake, organisation where there is no masterful director, books where the author has disappeared, painting where some accomplished brush paints with an equal pleasure, or with a bored impartiality, the human form or an old bottle, dirty weather and clean sunshine.
> . . . men, for the first time since the seventeenth century, see the world as an object of contemplation, not as something to be remade, and some few, meeting the limit in their special study, even doubt if there is any common experience, doubt the possibility of science.
>
> (AV 300)

'Synthesis for its own sake, organisation where there is no masterful director, books where the author has disappeared': one discerns the outlines of Eliot and Pound, the paths Yeats tried not to take. He was trying to resist the imminent 'general surrender of the will', but it may be that his rearguard action to stave it off was less honest and less effective than a less 'masterful' approach might have been.

Such thoughts as these may be behind Yeats's proposal at the end of this poem finally to surrender the will, to lie down in a landscape which reflects twentieth-century exhaustion and his own, an exhaustion which he had tried to conceal during his life but is now prepared to accept, almost to welcome.

Though memorable in several respects, Yeats's performance on this occasion is not completely convincing: it is too rhetorical, too abstract, too hyperbolic — particularly for a poem whose subject is the renunciation of such large gestures. But its theme is undoubtedly genuine, and the poem that fails to express it is an important one. One might say that the landscape of 'old kettles, old bottles, and a broken can' lies on the border of Yeats country, and therefore his attempt to occupy it in this poem was bound to fail. Its present tenant is Samuel Beckett, whose ladder may be the last to start from such squalor, a ladder built upon the conviction that there are no more ladders — or as Clov puts it, no more pain-killer.

Purgatory (1938) and the Last Plays

In his marvellous prologue to the *Death of Cuchulain* Yeats says 'I am old, I belong to mythology'; and indeed all of his last five plays are mythopoeic. *Purgatory* is certainly the best of these, and one is not surprised to learn that he announced from the stage of the Abbey Theatre after its premiere that he had filled it with his 'own conviction about this world and the next'.[16]

In *A Full Moon in March* and *The King of the Great Clock Tower* we find quite straightforward treatments of the Salome motif. The queen is in her castle, bored with the exhaustive state of her power and beauty. The problem which absolute monarchs share with Salome figures is narcissism, the absence of otherness through and against which to define the self.[17] Although in *A Full Moon* the queen appropriately

16.   Cited in V. Moore's *Unicorn*, p. 427.

17.   Cf. Hegel: 'For these persons [the Caesars] find themselves in a position in which they cannot be said to act, since no object confronts them in opposition: they have only to will — well or ill — and it *is* so' (*Philosophy of History*, p. 316). Yeats compresses: 'What had the Caesars but their thrones?' (CP 210).

enough emphasizes her virginity, the lady in the *Clock Tower* clearly has a husband and is therefore only intact in the spiritual sense. In both plays the deathly silence at court is broken by the intrusion of a rough beast, a manifestly sacred fool figure whose severed head possesses and is possessed by the devastated queen.

As in the fairy tales, the queen may be the incarcerated maiden awaiting the penetrating deliverance of her knight errant — though of course the dialectic is everywhere drawing out its contradictions and so it is a tale for grown-ups. More specifically, she symbolizes an exhaustively articulate European civilization awaiting with terrified desire the shattering arrival of a new dispensation which, as Yeats has tirelessly pointed out, must come from beneath. In the second play she is also the imperfect flesh which is to be consumed and renewed in the refining fires of alchemical poetry. But in the end these are almost friendly circus animals: *Purgatory* is altogether more frightening, as it suggests that the European imagination is broken beyond repair.

*

Although Salome does not appear in *Purgatory,* one can find her in the old man's mother, an aristocratic lady who married the stable-groom, an act symbolic of the destruction of Georgian Ireland and hence implicitly of European civilization itself. What is immediately striking is that this old man, whose counterpart in the *Death of Cuchulain* seemed quite convinced and not fastidious about the need for 'severed heads', here takes the strongest possible exception to his mother's action and sees in it no promise of renewal:

> to kill a house
> Where great men grew up, married, died,
> I here declare a capital offence.

And yet this old man, who has a very intense concern for his mother, puts the blame on his father, the groom: 'But he killed the house.' We know this cannot be so, however, for by all that Yeats holds sacred, political and cultural responsibility resides in the aristocracy, not in the lower orders, which when brutalized cannot be expected to be anything but wanton and rapacious; indeed one might see in this tale the undoing of a perfectly wholesome stable-groom by the unnatural lusts of a randy lady. The ambiguity in the situation bears comparison with Hamlet's paralysing uncertainty over the extent to which Gertrude's lust was responsible for the destruction of a house by a usurping lecher who ought not to have been in his mother's bed.

At the age of sixteen the old man had murdered his father amongst the flames consuming their great house — flames which the father had kindled in a drunken moment to complete the destruction begun on his wedding day (his wife having died in childbirth). By killing his father the son hoped to punish a great crime, remove the usurper, and placate the ghost of his mother. And yet as Oedipus discovered, to kill a father is not to become him but to destroy him in oneself, and thereby to disqualify oneself from the possession of one's mother. To put it another way, parricide, like the crucifixion of Christ, is self-defeating when the assassin recognizes that he has attempted to deny his source, his own authority; at which point he becomes perpetually obliged to imitate the father, to resurrect the self he has denied. Thus instead of burying the father, one is continuously trying to disinter him; and if one killed him as a false father, as one who either illegitimately possessed one's mother or never really did so, the attempt to resurrect him becomes ludicrous. It seems a quite convincing version of hell.

In *Purgatory* the old man may be tacitly recognizing this web of implication when he says:

I ran away, worked here and there
Till I became a pedlar on the roads,
No good trade, but good enough
Because I am my father's son,
Because of what I did or may do.

In the passages which follow, it becomes clear that the old man is obsessed by the act of his own conception, and its attempted reproduction in the conception of his son.

If one accepts that procreation is the planting of oneself in another, then one's child is both self and other. *Qua* self the child embodies and preserves one's substance. But the self of this old man was polluted by parricide and cannot resurrect the father through the son; that is, he cannot become his father by having a son. Consequently the son he would father must register *his* essential fatherlessness as best he can — in this case with a knife perhaps, had the old man not done so first.

Qua other, one's child represents the alien element into which one has risked oneself: at once an offer of immortality and of obliteration. By murdering his son at the moment he acquires vision and becomes a 'free' moral agent (that is, both self and other), the old man is attempting not only to preserve himself from obliteration at the hands of the other, but also to end the consequence of his family pollution, to purge *miasma* by offering a blood sacrifice to the gods.

Having spent his whole life living rough with the old man, the boy can find in his father's descriptions of the old Georgian culture only the strangeness of faery tale: 'My God but you had luck! Grand clothes, and maybe a grand horse to ride.' But though the abstract cultural argument escapes him, its cutting edge does not:

> What if I killed you? You killed my grand-dad,
> Because you were young and he was old.
> Now I am young and you are old.

The old man admits he is mad, and he must remain deaf to the boy's words; for they would both distract him from his obsession and provide him with a disturbingly unheroic interpretation of it. But though the full complexity of his motives is hidden from him, their simple consequences are not:

> I stuck him with a knife,
> The knife that cuts my dinner now.

Theophagy is fundamental to the occidental imagination, and the old man has been daily reminded of his unholy communion at supper time. It is arguably this kind of honesty that has driven him mad. In any case he bears little resemblance to the voyeurs in 'Parnell's Funeral' who could neither admit the deed nor eat the heart; and we can be sure that when he goes off at the end to 'tell my old jokes among new men', he will still be cutting his daily bread with the jack-knife, 'my father and my son on the same jack-knife'.[18]

18. Cf. the blind old beggar-man in *The Death Of Cuchulain,* who kills the king with the knife that 'cuts my food' (CPL 702).

*

Purgatory is concerned with the most dangerous and palpable aspect of cultural transmission, the training of children. Virtually all of the poems examined in this book are concerned with the purging of cultural ideals, memories that run in the blood, a task which the poet's word-magic can confront with some confidence. And yet such confidence tends to ignore the fact that while we kill off our ancestral fathers by dismantling the constructs of culture, nature impels us, as ever, to produce children, who seek from us such constructs as we labour to dismantle in ourselves. It is an appalling dilemma (which, as we have seen, Yeats rarely dwells on); for either we meet their demands, and attempt to pass on to them a culture we try to kill in ourselves (an insane self-contradiction), or we ignore their demands, and persist in our purgative meditations. Either way we fail them; for without the loving discipline of a mother and a father, sanely grounded in a social context, a child's anarchic instincts cannot be successfully informed.

This dilemma need rarely be faced nowadays, however; for in our technologized society, mechanisms of various kinds have largely relieved parents from the responsibility of nurturing cultural ideals, and such mechanisms usually prevent the anarchy guaranteed by parental failure from becoming manifest. But if the machinery is allowed to break down (as it does now and then), the anarchy and the residue of our cultural conflicts become visible again. Yeats's vision was as free of machinery as any in the twentieth century, and in *Purgatory* he presents his view of the generation gap unmediated by mechanical opiates. It amounts to murder. The difference between him and us is that he was enough of a Victorian still to believe that fathers were strong enough to kill their children: 'Children dazed or dead!' (CP 273). Today we are probably more disposed to fear that it is the children who kill the fathers.[19] In either case, this conflict lies at the hidden centre of twentieth-century experience, at the point where poetic language is silenced by someting beyond it, and death ceases to be a metaphor. It is a proof of Yeats's vigour that, as an old man lusting for 'the ill breeding, the barbarism of truth' (L 903), he finally met this conflict head-on.

19.   Or rather, unfathered children will, when the machinery breaks down, kill for food and for whimsy. Doris Lessing explores this nightmare with chilling conviction in her *Memoirs of a Survivor* (London, Octagon Press, 1974). Cf. also William Burroughs, *The Wild Boys*, London, Calder and Boyars, 1972.

Purgatory is profoundly pessimistic because it sees no way in which European man can escape the wrath of his ancestral fathers. Our civilization was polluted by a crime which has passed from father to son through blood which requires the re-enactment of that crime in each generation; and without religious forms we cannot hope for release through ritual catharsis. The obvious response to this dilemma is to ignore it in the hope that it will go away; and this indeed is what we do. Most 'intelligent' citizens today, for example, could not find themselves in Yeats's *Purgatory*, and any inventory of modern energies will show that most of them (American above all) are based upon the ignorance or destruction of the past. It is, of course, unlikely that the gods can be so easily outwitted, and we shall perhaps soon be called to account for the estrangement that has settled almost everywhere.

That, however, is another story. Our concern here is with the last perverse and heroic attempts to get the answers right, to recognize pollution and seek some resolution of it. With the churches closed and the theatres languishing, the prospects for ritual catharsis look bleak. The only real possibility is to follow Hamlet's example and attempt to break the inheritance by calling for no more marriages; but this requires an almost saintly degree of disciplined nihilism that is beyond the capacities of most. In Hamlet's case it led to a crazy lady and a bloodbath; and in the case of *Purgatory* it led to a bastard son 'got upon a tinker's daughter in a ditch' (CPL 684). In Samuel Beckett's *Endgame* Hamm tries to outwit the curse by taking in a local peasant's son. But it does not work: the blood that calls for a new generation, however illegitimate, revives the curse.

And yet, though the curse revives in each generation, one would expect its power to dwindle as cultural memory fragments and fades. This dwindling is registered in *Purgatory* by the tinker's daughter: her blood is not animated by the memories which drive the old man, and one would therefore expect her son to be less infected than his father. And indeed this is so; for he resists his father's instruction: 'No, you are mad! You are getting madder every day' (CPL 685). But in the end the father's will prevails, and just as the boy sees the light, his father stabs him.

Thus Yeats has tried to indicate that pollution of this kind is gradually dispersed through history. What is acted out in the first generations becomes maddening fantasy in the subsequent ones, and finally in the boy, a desire not to know where he came from. The ideas are right, as old as Greek tragedy, but Yeats's handling of this declension in *Purgatory* is rather crude: there is not enough bad blood between father and son to call forth such savagery, and one senses authorial wilfulness in the son's murder.

Beckett resolves this problem in *Endgame*. Hamm is too old, too lost in memory to kill Clov, who in any case is only his adopted son; and Clov, who cannot remember his 'real' father, cannot get close enough to Hamm really to touch him. All they can do is define the dislocation of the filial bond, the absence of connection:

Hamm: I was never there.
Clov: Lucky for you.
Hamm: Absent, always. It all happened without me. I
         don't know what's happened.

Here as elsewhere Beckett completes the work Yeats could not finish.

'The Black Tower' (1939)

Written a week before he died, this is Yeats's last poetic testament. Like most of his best works it is a ghost story; and it is addressed to the spirits which his poetry has tried to propitiate.

A number of men live in the old black tower, among them perhaps the old man from *Purgatory*, oath-bound to resist the banners of the new order that 'come to bribe or threaten'. The setting is medieval, but there is no trace of Pre-Raphaelite softness in the astringent language and spare abstract strokes which compose the picture. Although the language is unsettlingly abstract it is also quite astoundingly particular; indeed it offers another example of the 'paratactic' style (discussed on page 112) which Yeats occasionally mastered in his later poems, and which is fully revived in the works of Beckett. The strange situation invoked in the first stanza becomes even more bizarre when one realizes in the second that the siege is taking place only in the minds of the tower's occupants. Banners which can 'whisper' and even interrogate are not actually fluttering beyond the walls, but are part of an internal drama in which the mind questions the sanity of its allegiances. In fact the new king is probably indifferent to the harmless cranks in the black tower; indeed he may not even know they exist. This makes their determination to remain on guard almost unbearably foolish.

What makes such foolishness bearable is the sound in the refrain of old bones shaking in the mountain tomb. These are the bones of the dead king and his courtiers. That the bones shake when the wind roars means they are unquiet in the grave, not yet at peace, neither forgiving nor forgiven; and this keeps the black tower occupied.

The third stanza appears even more bizarre until one realizes that the cook represents the body which is aged by its labours to keep itself going, whereas the 'hale men' represent the ageless mind whose only business is with the shaking bones. From the body's point of view this mind is asleep, and seems either self-possessed or stupidly drugged. The mind, for reply, resists the body and its sensuous demands which would tempt it out of its tower and back to the world of banners and good food.

The situation is reproduced with extraordinary similarity in Beckett's *Endgame,* where the body (Clov) tries to convince the mind (Hamm) that there is life outside its tower, and that Hamm's determination to stay inside remembering old stories is insanely self-destructive. To this Hamm replies that it is impossible to leave, because without its memories the mind would simply cease to exist. Beckett's play is one of the few major works of literature to appear since Yeats's death, and though its rhetoric is manifestly post-Yeatsian, it tacitly recognizes that the old man was not nearly as out of touch as many would have us believe.

To understand the image of shaking bones one must look at the preceding poem, 'Cuchulain Comforted', written a week before and even more eerie. When the dead Cuchulain goes underground, he has left the world but has not yet become a shade: he still requires the rites of passage which will take him through purgatory to his final destination. In the alchemical terms of 'Byzantium' (introduced above on page 28) he is a receding image of 'unpurged day', more man than shade. Because the blood has not been purged he is still 'violent and famous', still tending 'to meditate on wounds and blood'. The crucial term here is 'famous', for it is his fame, which persists in the memory of the living, that still ties him to the world.

Milton said that fame is 'the last infirmity of noble mind', and Yeats would agree with him here. It is infirm because it is part of the dramatic illusion which sustains the worldly play. A man's fame is the power others give him because they think him powerful. Fame then, though something mental, is an aspect of power, which is 'like everything which has the stain of blood, a property of the living'; and it must be shed if we are to attain that wisdom which is 'the property of the dead, a something incompatible with life' (CP 269).

What that wisdom reveals is that 'we are convicted cowards all'. This statement should not be taken as radically nihilistic but rather as pointing to the fact that all men, however splendid their fame, live in the fear of death and in search of a home the world cannot furnish. This knowledge is what fame and the desire for it obscure, and until it has been grasped the shade of Cuchulain must 'stride' among the dead, meditating on wounds and blood.

This meditation takes place in purgatory, but also in the purgatorial region of those living minds where the fame of Cuchulain is still remembered. Indeed it is above all in the minds of the living, for in Yeats's theology it is the living who must bury the dead.[20] What must be recalled in this meditation is both the heroism and the cowardice of Cuchulain, the life and the death, the illusion and the reality. When this is done, he may 'lie down and die' (CP 393); having been remembered he may be forgotten; having finally come to know himself, he may forget himself. This moment of transfiguration is symbolized here, as is usual with Yeats, by his changing into a bird.

In this poem the purgatorial process (which is the theological term for the alchemical poetry Yeats has tried to write) is represented by the sewing of a shroud. The shades who have already been refined ('more image than a shade') urge Cuchulain to begin with his because in his unpurged state he is a source of unease — 'The rattle of those bones makes us afraid'. Until he is shrouded he lives on in the minds of the living, inflaming their blood with the need to imitate his fame. In short he is a mythic memory, who inspires men to go and

20. The clearest statement of this belief comes near the end of *The Resurrection* where he says 'God and man die each other's life, live each other's death' (CPL 594).

do likewise. As culture-hero he animates the lives of those who revere him until the purgatorial process is complete. When it is, the story is over, for it has been told.

And when the story is over, what then? When all the ghosts who have haunted Yeats's ancestral tower have been laid to rest, he too is effectively dead, for his blood is no longer moved by memory: 'We free ourselves from obsession that we may be nothing. The last kiss is given to the void.'[21] The man who can bestow this kiss is the saint, of whom Yeats says: 'His joy is to be nothing, to do nothing, to think nothing; but to permit the total life, expressed in its humanity, to flow in upon him and to express itself through his acts and thoughts' (AV 180). The saint is the proper 'hero' of a civilization on the verge of self-destruction, according to Yeats, and if he has left us anything to hope for and bend ourselves towards, it must be this.

The possibility of saintliness did not arise for Yeats himself because, as 'The Black Tower' indicates, the ghosts kept him busy until the end. Like the church today, this tower is a lonely place where prayers are said. It is also the poet's mind which remains bound to the still troubled spirits of his ancestral fathers. Until their deaths and the passing of what they fought for has been successfully shrouded in poetry which recognizes that it had to be so and is well that it was so, the bones will shake. In the poem's last line, though the dead no longer 'stand upright', the bones are still shaking.

Most people today cannot hear them; but those that can must listen. Not unlike the ghost of Hamlet's father, they are saying 'Remember me'. To remember them involves not only publishing the true story of how they lived and died but also accepting in ourselves what they have truly left us. In the past ten years the only lively activity in the occidental black tower has come from the disaffected children of the affluent middle classes who have returned to the land in order to retrieve the discipline and piety of a natural life. In burying false fathers they hope to disinter the spirits of fathers murdered long ago. To fight parricide with parricide is a desperate undertaking, and largely for historical reasons it has prospered most in America, where the presence of Indian ghosts has facilitated the attempt to recognize and purge the parricidal pollution in which that society was conceived.

21.   Letter to T. Sturge Moore, 17 April 1929.

Needless to say, the chances of actually *resurrecting* ancient pieties in such a maddened world cannot be many. Less ambitious is the ultimately oriental aspiration behind Yeats's poetry, to 'free ourselves from obsession that we may be nothing'. Those of us who attempt this are hoping that when the bones have been shrouded we may forget them, leave the black tower, and perhaps find the new banners less threatening than we had supposed. For this to succeed we must be able to learn from the East how to live without history. Against this possibility one must set the appalling pessimism of Beckett's Hamm, that if we leave the black tower we leave those memories through which alone we can know ourselves to be human; and the machine is waiting to collect us.

The past is certainly about to die; but is there a future to be born? The mystery of death and re-birth is as ancient as can be, and its invocation here may fittingly conclude this contemporary story.

BIBLIOGRAPHY OF WORKS CITED

Erich Auerbach   *Mimesis*, Princeton, Princeton University Press, 1953.

Hannah Arendt   *The Human Condition*, New York, Anchor, 1959. (HC)

Samuel Beckett   *Endgame*, London, Faber, 1965.

Walter Benjamin   *Illuminations*, New York, Schocken, 1969.

William Blake   *The Poetry and Prose of William Blake* (ed. Keynes), London, Nonesuch, 1961. (B)

F. H. Bradley   *Essays on Truth and Reality*, Oxford, Clarendon Press, 1914.

Kenneth Clark (ed.)   *Ruskin Today*, Harmondsworth, Penguin Books, 1967.

David Cooper (ed.)   *Dialectics of Liberation*, Harmondsworth, Penguin Books, 1968.

Richard Ellmann   *Yeats: The Man and the Masks*, London, Faber, 1961. (MM)
The Identity of Yeats, London, Faber, 1964.

James Frazer   *The Golden Bough*, London, Macmillan, 1922.

Northrop Frye   *Fearful Symmetry*, Princeton, Princeton University Press, 1947.

Peter Gay   *The Party of Humanity*, London, Weidenfeld and Nicolson, 1964.

E. H. Gombrich   *Meditations on a Hobby Horse*, London, Phaidon, 1963.
The Story of Art, London, Phaidon, 1964.

Robert Graves   *The White Goddess*, London, Faber, 1961.

Ronald Gray   *The German Tradition in Literature, 1871-1945*, Cambridge University Press, 1965.

G. W. F. Hegel   *Aesthetik*, Berlin, Aufbau-Verlag, 1955.
Philosophy of History (trans. Sibree), New York, Dover, 1954.

G. W. F. Hegel	*The Phenomenology of Mind*, London, Allen & Unwin, 1931.
Erich Heller	*The Artist's Journey into the Interior*, London, Secker and Warburg, 1966.
Joseph Hone	*W. B. Yeats*, London, Macmillan, 1965. (WBY)
Henri Hubert and Marcel Mauss	*Sacrifice: Its Nature and Function*, London, Cohen and West, 1964.
A. N. Jeffares	*W. B. Yeats: Man and Poet*, London, Routledge and Kegan Paul, 1962.
	A Commentary on the Collected Poems of W. B. Yeats, London, Macmillan, 1968. (C)
and K. G. W. Cross (eds.)	*In Excited Reverie*, London, Macmillan, 1965. (IER)
Walter Kaufmann	*Hegel*, New York, Doubleday, 1965.
Frank Kermode	*The Romantic Image*, London, Routledge and Kegan Paul, 1957. (RI)
Claude Levi-Strauss	*Totemism* (trans. R. Needham), London, Merlin Press, 1964.
Thomas Mann	*Letters to Paul Amann*, London, Secker and Warburg, 1961.
Vivian Mercier	*The Irish Comic Tradition*, London, Chatto and Windus, 1962.
George Moore	*Hail and Farewell*, London, Heinemann, 1914 (vol. I, *Ave*, vol. II, *Salve*, vol. III, *Vale*).
Virginia Moore	*The Unicorn*, New York, Macmillan, 1954.
Desmond Morris	*The Naked Ape*, London, Corgi, 1968.
Friedrich Nietzsche	*The Birth of Tragedy and the Genealogy of Morals* (trans. Golffing), New York, Anchor, 1956. (BT).
	The Will to Power (trans. Kaufmann), New York, Vintage, 1968.
Frank O'Connor	*Kings, Lords, and Commons*, London, Macmillan, 1962.
Mario Praz	*The Romantic Agony*, London, Fontana, 1960.
I. A. Richards	*Beyond*, New York, Harcourt Brace Jovanovich, 1974

Bertrand Russell	*Autobiography*, vol. II, London, Allen and Unwin, 1968.
Jon Stallworthy	*Between the Lines*, Oxford University Press, 1963.
Hugh Staples (ed.)	*The Ireland of Sir Jonah Barrington*, London, Peter Owen, 1968.
Donald Torchiana	*W. B. Yeats and Georgian Ireland*, Evanston, Northwestern University Press, 1966.
W. B. Yeats	*Collected Poems*, London, Macmillan, 1961. (CP)
	Collected Plays, London, Macmillan, 1963. (CPL)
	Autobiographies, London, Macmillan, 1956. (A)
	Mythologies, London, Macmillan, 1962. (M)
	Essays and Introductions, London, Macmillan, 1961. (EI)
	Explorations, London, Macmillan, 1962. (E)
	A Vision, New York, Macmillan, 1961. (AV)
	Letters, ed. Allan Wade, London, Rupert Hart-Davis, 1954. (L)
	Variorum Edition of the Poems, ed. Allt and Alspach, New York, Macmillan, 1957. (V)
	Letters on Poetry to Dorothy Wellesley, Oxford University Press, 1964. (LDW)
and Shree Purohit Swami (trans.)	*The Ten Principal Upanishads*, London, Faber, 1970.

Q7